ANDREW TODHUNTER

DANGEROUS GAMES

Andrew Todhunter lives in Northern California.
He is also author of *Fall of the Phantom Lord.*

ALSO BY ANDREW TODHUNTER

Fall of the Phantom Lord

DANGEROUS GAMES

ANCHOR BOOKS

A DIVISION OF RANDOM HOUSE, INC.

NEW YORK

DANGEROUS
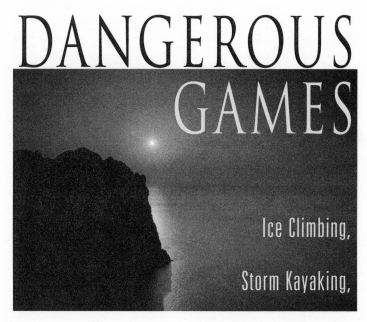
GAMES

Ice Climbing,

Storm Kayaking,

and Other Adventures

from the

Extreme Edge of Sports

ANDREW
TODHUNTER

FIRST ANCHOR BOOKS EDITION, NOVEMBER 2001

Copyright © 2000 by Andrew Todhunter

Some of these stories were first published as follows: A version of "The Seam" first appeared in the September 2000 issue of *National Geographic Adventure*. Reprinted with permission of *National Geographic*. "The Last Voyage of Steve Sinclair" combines two articles: "Gale Force Kayaking" in the August 1995 issue of *The Atlantic Monthly* and "Paddling Out: The Last Voyage of Steve Sinclair" in the August 1996 issue of *Sea Kayaker*. "Beneath the Ice" first appeared in the January 1994 issue of *The Atlantic Monthly*. "Dark Passage" first appeared in the July 1998 issue of *The Atlantic Monthly*. "The Precipitous World of Dan Osman" first appeared in the January 1996 issue of *The Atlantic Monthly*. "Stillwater" first appeared as "Incident at Stillwater" in the October 1995 issue of *Men's Journal*. "The Wreck of the *Belle*" first appeared as "Diving into the Wreck" in the July/August 1996 issue of *Preservation*, the magazine of the National Trust for Historic Preservation. "The Taming of the Saw" first appeared in the January 1995 issue of *The Atlantic Monthly*. "On Cannon Cliff" first appeared in the November 1999 issue of *The Atlantic Monthly*.

Title page photograph courtesy of PhotoDisc, Inc.

The Library of Congress has cataloged the Doubleday edition as follows:
Todhunter, Andrew.
Dangerous games: ice climbing, storm kayaking, and other adventures from the extreme edge of sports / Andrew Todhunter.—1st ed.
p. cm.
1. Athletes—United States—Biography. 2. Extreme sports—United States.
3. Risk-taking (Psychology) I. Title.
GV697.A1 T63 2000
796'.092'273—dc21
[B]
99-087492

ANCHOR ISBN: 0-385-48644-8

Author photograph © Erin Todhunter
Book design by Amanda Dewey

www.anchorbooks.com

Printed in the United States of America
10 9 8 7 6 5 4 3 2 1

In memory of
Dan Osman and Steve Sinclair

CONTENTS

DANGEROUS GAMES

THE SEAM

In October of 1982, a twenty-seven-year-old British alpinist named Alex MacIntyre was killed by rock fall during a descent of the south face of Annapurna. Another British climber named John Porter was at base camp, watching the descent through his camera. MacIntyre and French alpinist René Ghilini were retreating after a failed attempt on the summit. "They were down climbing," Porter describes, "crossing a gully on a face that was the better part of ten thousand feet high. I lowered the camera to clean a speck of dust off the lens, and when I looked up again, René was alone on the face." MacIntyre had been struck and killed instantly by a single falling stone; his body tumbled to a ledge 500 feet below.

Nearly seventeen years later, Porter drives through the darkness north of Glasgow, Scotland. It is the middle of March, and we're headed into the Scottish highlands for four days of ice and alpine climbing. Porter is preparing to write a biography of MacIntyre, and the events of 1982 have been much on his mind.

Porter was one of the finest mountaineers of his generation; MacIntyre, eight years younger, had been his protégé. Classmates at Leeds University, they were also good friends. Porter, MacIntyre, and other British climbers of the so-called "Leeds scene" led a renaissance of British alpinism beginning in the late 1970s. Before expeditions, MacIntyre's mother told Porter, "Take care of my boy." Eventually, Porter says, MacIntyre outstripped his tutor. In MacIntyre's obituary, Porter wrote, without envy but with a certain fraternal sadness, of the moment he realized that he had nothing more to offer; that his pupil had grown up and surpassed him. Around 1980, Reinhold Messner, arguably the greatest mountaineer of all time, lauded MacIntyre as the purest proponent of Himalayan superalpinism then at work. Messner was referring to a stylistic school of mountaineering that favors fast, light climbs by small teams or soloists—a style, born in the Alps, that Messner introduced to the Himalayas have formed the crucible of modern ice climbing. In the 1950s and '60s, says Porter, "the Scots used to say they went climbing in the Alps to train for winter climbing in Scotland. The technical difficulty of these small mountains, together with the severe conditions, made them an ideal testing ground for aspiring alpinists. Most of Britain's finest high-altitude climbers trace their successes to winters spent in the Scottish hills."

We leave a car in the crowded parking lot of the Cairngorm Ski Area before 9 A.M., hike past the chair lifts, and join a broken file of climbers meandering up a bare, rocky incline toward the peaks. While the terrain is bare of trees, a coarse, wind-combed heather clings to the frozen mud. This soon vanishes beneath the snow as we ascend. Studded here and there by rocks sheathed in hoarfrost, the surface of the snow glitters with a crust of ice.

An hour's hike from the car lies Coire an t-Sneachda, a popular ravine, or "corrie." Reminiscent of Tuckerman's Ravine on the lower slopes of New Hampshire's Mount Washington, the corrie is shaped like a three-sided bowl, enclosed by massive, rocky buttresses and steep snow slopes prone to avalanche. Rim to rim, the corrie is some two and a half miles in diameter; its floor lies nearly 1,000 feet beneath its crest. In heavy gusts, a cold wind scours the floor of the ravine with spindrift, a dry, granular snow that lashes exposed skin and gathers like fine sand in an opened pack. We halt at the base of a crag identified in the climbers' guidebook as Aladdin's Buttress and sort our gear. Nearby, other groups of climbers do likewise. On a shallow rise near the base of the buttress stands a weathered plastic first-aid kit the size of a steamer trunk.

Despite the corrie's low altitude, the winter conditions make for alpine climbing—a mix of rock, ice, and snow climbing first developed in the Alps. For the cold, over layers of synthetic underwear, we wear waterproof jackets and pants, lined gloves, alpine climbing boots, and hats, or balaclavas. Harnesses follow, then crampons—metal frames, equipped with filed teeth for traction on ice, strapped to the soles of our boots. Each climber carries at least two short-shafted ice tools (or modified ice axes), and most have a third in reserve. The threat of rock and ice fall in alpine climbing requires a helmet.

We ascend the steep snowfield at the foot of Aladdin's Buttress and find two parties waiting at the base of our intended route: Aladdin's direct, a short, near-vertical wall of hard water ice that tops out into a gully. The climbers decide on a more difficult alternative: Patey's Route, a classic gully climb first led by local climbing legend Tom Patey in February of 1959. Until his rock-climbing death in 1970, Patey was the archetypal Scottish winter climber, assailing the most challenging lines of the day, often in terrible weather, with little more in the way of equipment than a pair of battered ice tools and crampons. Photographs of Patey usually show a man dressed for a trip to the woodpile, with a bare head, torn sweater, and wool mittens that resemble snowballs. It's enough to make you wonder if he's wearing socks. More often than not in such photographs, the grinning Patey is 1,000 feet up a howling gully, climbing at the edge of the grade. A country doctor by profession, Patey also wrote some of the liveliest prose on climbing to be found. While the technical difficulty of his route on Aladdin's Buttress has retreated before forty years of advances in technique and technology, the gully remains a solid intermediate climb at Grade 5. As we prepare our ropes, another party rappels off the route, defeated, they report, by "thin" ice conditions.

Unlike pure ice climbing, popularized by photographs of climbers on frozen waterfalls, much of the winter climbing in Scotland is "mixed," a hybrid of ice, snow, exposed rock, and occasionally frozen turf. On such a route, a climber will alternate between ice- and rock-climbing techniques, often in close sequence. On rock, this commonly entails "dry tooling," hooking or wedging ice tools and crampon points on small ledges and in cracks.

With the previous party safely out of the gully, Hall ties one end of a rope to his harness and starts up, belayed by Rhodes. The two climbers are soon at the next ledge, and Porter starts up the gully while I belay. As he climbs, Porter seeks horns or cracks in the rock or patches of hard ice where he may place pieces of protection, small devices designed to arrest a climber's fall.

Porter has soon joined the others and calls for me to follow.

The route starts up a deep, V-shaped chimney, or notch, the rock covered with snow. As I climb, I clear the dry snow off the rocks with my tools and forearms, revealing the holds beneath. I peck with the picks in the glazed cracks, seeking the deepest ice before planting the tools with solid strokes. Farther up the chimney lie small patches of frozen turf, tucked between the rocks under the snow. Picks and front-points seat readily in this granular cement of grass and mud, which is less prone than ice to shatter or shear. The wind gusts erratically up and down the chimney, driving the powder before it. The spindrift is often inescapable; when I bow my head to avoid a long, dense blast from above, a gust snaps up between my boots and dashes my face with snow. In the heaviest gusts, one has little choice but to lean into the chimney and seal the hood entirely with a gloved hand. In such moments, in the damp darkness, warmed by your breath, you can feel the buffeting wind and the spindrift pouring down from above as if through an hourglass, hissing like a downpour of the finest rain.

Two pitches later, we top out of the gully at four o'clock. Here at the corrie's rim, on the edge of the Cairngorm plateau, the wind gusts up to fifty miles per hour. Studded with rocks, the plateau rolls away into the grey distance. The plateau is far more dangerous, says Hall, than the gullies behind us. In Scotland, more climbers die from exposure than by any other means. Hikers are at equal risk; some years ago, a schoolteacher and nine children were fatally caught in a whiteout on this plateau, within sight of our position on the corrie's rim.

We rise earlier the following morning and drive in two cars to another site, Creag Meagaidh, an hour to the west. It drizzles intermittently en route, and as Porter pulls into the lot and parks beside Hall, it is raining steadily. The avalanche danger will be too great on Creag Meagaidh, Hall says, given the rain. On the drive over, Hall and Rhodes heard news on the radio of a death yesterday on Ben Nevis, the highest peak in the British Isles at 1,343 meters, or 4,406 feet. We intend to climb the Ben at some point in the next three days. A man and woman, high on a route called Point Five Gully, were hit by a heavy spindrift avalanche and swept nearly 2,000 feet to the gully's base. Miraculously, in one of the longest survived falls on the Ben, the woman lived with a broken neck and other injuries. Her partner was killed. Porter later tells me that ten or twenty climbers are killed every winter in Scotland—as many as thirty or forty in a bad year (by comparison, some thirty climbers die year round, on average, in all of North America). At the moment, sitting in a car in the rain, this seems like a great number of lives, year after year, to be lost for a day on the hill.

The climbers decide to return to Coire an t-Sneachda. In the highlands, the weather tends to improve toward the east, away from the Atlantic. We may get rained out there as well, but it's our only chance at a day. On the drive back, this theory seems to hold true. The rain steadily diminishes, until we arrive at the Cairngorm Ski Area under a broken blue and grey sky. Bad weather is a simple fact of Scottish climbing. If it rains or snows two out of three days in the east, says Porter, in the west it is three out of four. Climbers in Scotland for a week will feel lucky to get three clear days. Historically, the boldest native climbers have rarely been discouraged by heavy snowfall and have often climbed through blizzards. There are still some climbers who will tolerate the greatly increased risk of avalanche to savor the pleasures of climbing in such "full conditions," when spindrift streams incessantly down the frozen gullies, wind drowns out the shouts of other climbers, and little can be seen for the whiteout.

We arrive at the base of the corrie at ten forty-five and climb the snow slope past the foot of Patey's Route to the base of Aladdin's Mirror direct. Twenty-five meters in height, the Grade 4 route is described in the guide as "a popular ice problem, sometimes underestimated." Porter makes short, easy work of the ice wall, placing two ice screws for protection as he climbs. He belays from the foot of the snow gully above, and I follow, removing the screws as I pass them. While climbing, the follower, or "second," removes any gear placed by the leader and returns them at the next belay. If the climbers switch leads, the second (now the leader) may keep the gear and use it to protect the next pitch. In this fashion, I climb past Porter and up the gully to the next belay. From there we descend to the right, down the gentler snow gully of Aladdin's Mirror. We pass a party of three climbers, ascending the gully unroped. The last of them is clearly uncomfortable, and the party eventually backs off, passing us as we coil our ropes.

Porter and I pause for lunch on the corrie floor. Hall and Rhodes have gone ahead and can be seen halfway up the first pitch of our next route, a vertical chimney that cuts a black slash up the center of a rocky pyramid on the right flank of the Fiacaill Buttress.

From a distance, the Seam intimidates and beckons. It is the kind of natural line—striking, ominous, direct—that at first glance begs an attempt. While not the longest line in the corrie at 100 meters, and certainly not the most technically challenging at Grade 5, it may be the most visually compelling. Later, I am surprised to learn that it was first climbed in 1986, years after most of the gullies and chimneys in the corrie had been led. Before the rise of mixed climbing in the 1980s, Porter explains, the Seam was only considered a summer rock-climbing route; there is so little ice in the chimney that in Patey's day, climbers would have declared it out of condition and unclimbable in winter.

As we gather our gear and start across the corrie around two o'clock, the sky has clouded over and the wall of the Fiacaill Buttress lies in deep shadow. I feel a vague foreboding, a sense that something is going to go wrong on the route.

It's just the accident on Ben Nevis, I think, and stopping for lunch. I've been thinking about those climbers tumbling down Point Five, and sitting in the cold drains desire. The feeling remains, however, and as Porter and I start up the snow slope in the shadows, I'm consciously tired and cold. The worst thing about this apprehension, however murky it remains, is that it seems to involve one of the others—whom I can't say. The issue is further complicated by the fact that they're all much better climbers. I decide not to mention my concern and hope for the best.

It's two-thirty by the time we arrive at the first belay, and Porter seems pressed. With good reason, he doesn't want us stuck on the route—or on the ridge above—after dark. I belay him on the first pitch, a straightforward scramble up the steeper snow and rock to the foot of the chimney. By the time I join Porter at the second ledge, Rhodes has followed Hall up the chimney out of sight. Hall soon appears above, lowering down from the anchor above to shoot pictures. As he prepares to lead the chimney, Porter expresses fatigue. Hall and Rhodes have been climbing regularly, but Porter has never been on the route, and it's his first ice-climbing trip of the season. Rhodes has left Hall's hardware in place, and Porter may clip into them as he proceeds. He will still be leading, but the preplaced gear will save time. He sets off and soon starts up the chimney proper.

From my perspective, the chimney is exposed and daunting. Porter stops at an icy patchwork of cracked rock. He picks tentatively in the cracks with his tools, tries to get a foothold, steps down. He gazes up the chimney, and from his posture I can see he's out of sorts. He calls out that Hall and Rhodes have climbed out the ice in the cracks with their tools and crampons, that few decent placements remain. Minutes pass. He reaches up, pecks at a slot, withdraws the tool. He scrapes with his crampons and then steps down, ponders the chimney above. He's one of the world's most experienced mountaineers and at this moment he looks the way I feel—as if he'd rather be nearly anywhere else than right here, right now, on this climb. In another circumstance I might be comforted by the reminder that even the best have bad days, but at the moment my unease is rapidly descending into dread. If Porter's having trouble, how am I going to get up? I imagine getting caught halfway up the chimney, unable to proceed. Night falls like an axe, in this vision, and brings with it a storm.

"John," I call up to him. "Do me a favor and place a really bomber anchor for me when you get up there." Porter assures me that he will. Hall, leaning in his harness overhead, calls down with a kind of scolding encouragement. "Come on, John, you can climb this. Just place your tools. Don't keep moving them."

"It's my head," says Porter finally. "I've been thinking about extended family."

In our running conversation, I have been pressing Porter on the subject of climbing and responsibility, particularly if the climber in question has children. As the father of a two-year-old, I've been grappling with this subject a great deal. I suppose I hope to gain insight from a climber, like Porter, who has balanced a family and a career in mountaineering with great success. As it happens, these conversations may have succeeded in psyching us both out. If you think too much about climbing, about what your family stands to lose if you get killed, you may not climb for long, or with much enthusiasm. On the other hand, Porter may now be alive, to some degree, because he is naturally introspective. These are all issues that he has grappled with over the years, and he has backed off climbs that killed others who were equally competent. As prominent American alpinist John Bouchard puts it, "Porter knows when to fold his cards."

Porter finally gets up the first section, and Hall calls down, "That was the tricky part, John. The rest is easy." For a partner stuck on a route well within his ability, this is the classic ploy. From my angle, it looks like it gets a good deal harder. Porter will now move inside the chimney, on a steeper angle, with less ice and larger blocks that need to be surmounted.

Porter climbs on but continues to be tentative.

"Come on, John," calls Hall with more impatience. "You're thinking too much. You're not trusting your tools."

"I know that, Brian," says Porter, showing the first signs of irritation. "You don't need to tell me that."

He finally gets over the crux. This breaks the spell, and he begins to move faster. He is quickly off the route and out of sight. Relayed through Hall, Porter soon calls me to follow. The anchor cleaned, I cinch down the wrist straps on my tools and start up. With the luxury of an anchor overhead, I determine to climb fast and risk a fall. With Porter's belay overhead, I have nothing to lose. I face a far different climb, as a second, than did Porter and Hall. I'm also so cold that I'm eager to move quickly, regardless of its outcome. It's getting dark. I want off the buttress, and the only way off is up. All of this conspires, ironically, to my benefit. As an intermediate climber, expecting to fail, I throw myself at the route with resigned vigor. Lacking Porter's expertise, I know that if I stop to think I'm doomed. The climbing, in such a state of mind, comes more readily. A mix of thin ice placements in cracks, frontpointing on small ledges. The patchwork falls swiftly. I try to maintain a rapid, thoughtless pace, confident in the belay. In the chimney, I encounter a few moves where dropping the tools and using palm holds is easier than hooking with the picks. Warmed from exertion, climbing fast, I soon find myself happier to be climbing than I've ever been. Two-thirds of the way up, removing a piece, I realize that I'm rushing. I pause for a moment and breathe; I tell myself to relax, to pace myself. When I finally top out, I'm swearing in elation. In nearly twenty years of intermittent climbing, I have never felt such intense satisfaction in the mountains. For a few minutes, there on the ridge, I accept that it may be worth dying for.

We break down the anchors and hike up the ridge line while the sun sets over the mountains to the southwest. The climb's afterglow plateaus into reverence. The darkening sky is pink and teal. The crags, where bare of the snow, turn black. Despite the wind, there is a powerful sensation of expectant stillness. Porter takes one look at my expression and grins. "Nice, isn't it?" he says. We descend silently into the Coire and hike out to the car under Jupiter, which burns white as a star in the last field of blue sky to the west. Nearing the car, the tremendous high begins to ebb.

We drive west to Glencoe, stopping for a late dinner in Inverness-Shire. Then on to Glencoe and the famous Clachaig Inn (Clachaig means "Stony Place" in Gaelic), with an ice axe in lieu of a door handle and a brass plaque bolted to the front desk that reads NO HAWKERS OR CAMP-BELLS. We have a beer in the bar, followed by single-malt whiskeys in the sitting room. The walls of the lounge are covered with framed photographs of climbers, now dead. Porter, Hall, and Rhodes knew and climbed with many of them.

The following morning I wake to what appears from bed to be grey sky. Gulls cry in the distance; we are near the sea. Minutes later, the rain begins to patter on the corrugated tin roof outside my window; my sense of relief that this signals a rest day would be difficult to convey. We take a slow morning, then the four of us drive into the neighboring town of Fort William. In the drizzling rain, the town and shops are congested and depressing and somehow blasphemous after the climbing.

My spirits continue to sink throughout the day. We have dinner in the bar—or rather they do; I have lost my appetite. I retire early in the doldrums, dreading the possibility that we may climb tomorrow. I sit in my room and wonder if I can cancel the climb and get on a train.

The next morning I wake up numb but leveled off. I thumb through the guide and stumble on a Grade 5 route called *Vanishing Gully*. Two hundred meters high, the gully was first climbed in 1951. The guide describes it as a "classic ice climb, with good belays and protection." My desire to climb the Ben begins to rally. Porter knocks and enters.

"We had an idea," he says. "The conditions are probably going to be terrible. If getting to the top of the Ben is important to you, we could change plan and hike up the back. It would be a slog, and there wouldn't be any climbing, but we could almost certainly get you to the top." I have no interest in that and ask him about Vanishing Gully. "Can't do," he says. "The conditions will be awful as well as dangerous. But we might be able to go directly up Tower Ridge if the weather clears."

We gear up and drive to the parking lot near the Ben in Hall's car. It is drizzling and unseasonably warm. In these conditions, says Porter, everything on the Ben is getting washed out. But the weather may clear, so we pack for climbing and hike up across a boggy moor spotted with sheep. The mud is black with peat. The rain doesn't let up, and as we near the stone climbing hut, Porter says, apologetically, that there's no way we're going to climb.

A short distance above the cabin, near the foot of Tower Ridge, I build a small stone cairn in the rain. I have a small pouch of ashes in my pack—a portion of the ashes of a climber and friend who was killed in Yosemite Valley five months ago, leaving a twelve-year-old daughter and a fiancée. When I set off for Scotland, I had hoped to climb the Ben and scatter some of his ashes on its summit. Instead, I kneel and shake a portion of the ashes in a circle around the cairn. The wind snaps wisps of the fine grey powder into the air. In the ashes there are small shards, like arrowheads, of bleached bone.

In the evening we drive south through the hills, into England.

"When your friends die, you carry them with you," Porter says. "You collect their personalities, in a way, as you go on. And you're seeing things for them as much as for yourself. There's a fine line between carrying it around as baggage, as dead weight, and having it be something positive in your life. But they lived for climbing, and the only way they can continue to climb is through you. For that reason, you can't really stop climbing."

MacIntyre's death came in the midst of a rash of fatalities among Britain's top climbers. Peter Boardman and Joe Tasker, friends of Porter's, died on Everest earlier that year. Pete Thexton died on Broad Peak in 1983. Roger Baxter-Jones was killed by a falling serac, or ice tower, in the Alps in 1985. And there were others. "I was seeing something glorious become something very destructive," says Porter. For a couple of years, he considered getting out of the game.

In the end, he went back to it. "I needed those people, I needed the physical pleasure, I needed the potential for the sort of enlightenment that we had on the top of Cairngorm the other day. . . . Eternity is something you're faced with anyway, in this short span of years. The moments of insight you get from climbing are brief, but they encompass so much more than anything else I could do . . . So I had to go back. I had to find a way back in."

"So you realized that it was worth all of their lives and worth your own?" I asked him.

"Yes," he said.

In the mid-'80s, Porter climbed Mount Kenya's Diamond Couloir with Rhodes, attempted a new route on India's Shivling, and put up a first ascent on Kedar Dome, among others. His standard continued to improve. In 1986, he and Hall joined Al Rouse, another top British climber, and others on an attempt on the south face of K2, the world's second-highest and statistically most deadly peak. Climbing together, Porter and Rouse got close to the summit on an early push.

They had reached the summit ridge under clear skies, past the difficulties, and Porter voted to press on. But Rouse was the expedition leader and refused to summit before asking the others' permission. So they turned back. "That saved my life," says Porter, "and delayed Al's death by a month or so." A huge storm hit the summit hours later. Had they summited, both climbers would have almost certainly been killed on the descent. Weeks of bad weather followed, defeating subsequent attempts. After months on the mountain, Porter and Hall finally went home. Rouse remained, determined to summit. By the end of the season, Rouse and twelve others would be dead, victims to the deadliest year in K2's history.

In nearly four decades of climbing, Porter estimates that nearly half of the finest climbers he knew and climbed with were killed in the mountains. In military engagements, a fatality rate of 10 percent is considered a slaughter. Rarely, this figure is surpassed. Odds of fatality deduced over a lifetime differ greatly, of course, than odds deduced over a period of days or weeks. Nevertheless, Porter's estimate is devastating.

Over the last decade, the appearance of Porter's two children has dramatically altered his definition of acceptable risk. As a middle-aged husband and father, he suspects he won't be breaking any more new ground in the Himalayas, but he continues to climb.

"I'm not going to stop," he says. "There's no way, without denying your whole existence, that you can say, 'I'm going to quit this.' It's an addiction, in that way, but a very positive one. It gives your own life a greater value, but it also reinforces many other things that are crucial to the greater enjoyment of life, as you saw the other day.... It makes you believe in things which are much more powerful than you. It also makes you realize that to be too protective of anything is probably a mistake. You're not going to be here forever, and if you don't push it out, if you don't have those moments, then what will you have?

"All I can do now is climb at a level that gives me what I need in terms of a life, without being totally life-threatening, and without ever forgetting the fact that the mountain doesn't know you're an expert. At any time, there can be the single stone that plucks you off the face, there can be the loose hold, there can be the mistake in judgment. But you can do that with a lapse of concentration, changing a tape in a car."

We pull into Porter's driveway after dark. He lives with his family in a seventeenth-century stone farmhouse in a quiet village in the Lakes District. We pull our wet, mud-spattered gear out of the trunk, and he moves slowly to the front step, his gear hanging from his shoulders and in the crooks of his arms. The door bursts open suddenly, bathing him in yellow light. His daughters, aged six and nine, jump through the doorway with gleeful shouts. They nearly knock him down.

I am standing in the drive, gathering my gear, and from

my angle I can only see his profile as he bends down, burdened by his pack and boots and tools, and encircles his daughters with his arms. He looks relieved and tired and vaguely puzzled in the bright light, as if he doesn't know exactly how he of all of them escaped, and landed here, on this doorstep, alive.

THE LAST VOYAGE
OF STEVE SINCLAIR

Until recently, when the ocean rose and hurled itself against the towering sandstone cliffs of Elk, California, like a bull in a barn fire, and the spray, driven by the seventy-mile-per-hour wind, stripped the paint from the inns, the farmhouses, the church, and the Elk General Store, Steve Sinclair would duck his head through a narrow doorway and appear in the yard of a weathered shop, wearing a torn black wetsuit and an orange helmet, a double-bladed paddle in his hand.

It might be after three o'clock on a day in late December.

Sinclair has been digging trenches since early this morning. Known in the local construction community as a "human backhoe," he can dig a trench with a shovel faster than a machine-driven trenching tool. If you ask him how, he will leap from his chair and tell the story of an old Mexican laborer with hands worn smooth as vellum teaching the young Sinclair how to shovel without wasting his prodigious strength. Like most of Sinclair's stories, it is a tale you will not soon forget.

His boat, a nineteen-foot, fifty-eight-pound wash-deck torpedo called an Odyssea ski, lies strapped to a decomposing plywood rickshaw, its bow in the air. Lifting the tapered stern from the uncut grass, Sinclair wheels the vessel like a cannon along the dirt lane. The rickshaw's bicycle tires lie flat on rusted rims.

He pauses at the shoulder of Route One and peers through the rain in both directions for traffic, then crosses the road and turns down the long, rutted track from the height of the bluff to the beach of Greenwood Cove. The fiberglass hull shifts and creaks against the cross-cut plywood at every stone and gully.

Weaving a course through the driftwood high on the beach, Sinclair finally abandons the rickshaw, checks the boat's rudder cables and hatch covers, and moves down the beach, his paddle in one hand, his boat under his arm, its bow into the shrieking wind. Sinclair is six foot three and weighs 230 pounds. He stops and watches the shorebreak.

Fifteen- to twenty-foot faces explode on the beach every six seconds. The freezing rain rattles against the prow of his helmet like thrown gravel.

The last and largest wave of the set is rising. Beyond it lies a clearing, a window of time before the next set hits. Sinclair raises the boat above his head and starts to run, his paddle pinned to the deck beneath his thumb. At the precise moment that the wave hits the beach at his feet, Sinclair hurls his craft into the chaos of foam and vaults aboard. He paddles in long, deep strokes. He does not chop. He paddles fast but extends completely, reaching all the way forward, his chin between his knees. He follows through, driving from his feet, until he lies flat on his back against the hull, his arms nearly straight above his head. Before the next wave strikes, he has closed the distance and pierced its rising face.

He breaks seven lines of twenty-foot surf before passing Gunderson Rock, a 120-foot pyramid of sandstone a quarter mile offshore. Beyond Gunderson, outside the relative shelter of the cove, Sinclair encounters the groundswell—long, rolling mountainsides of green-black ocean, spray streaming from their crumbling tops like nets of white flame. The wind sings like corrugated steel being torn into strips. It rakes and pummels the surface of the water until the margin between sea and atmosphere is lost. To breathe, Sinclair must purse his lips and filter the air from the froth.

Sinclair refuses to estimate the size of the waves he

faces—from the paddler's vantage near the waterline, oceanic storm swells are too long, too broad for ordinary measurement. In any case, it is not their height as much as their
area—their "vast acreage" as Sinclair puts it—which daunts
him as he churns interminably in the direction of their
peaks. "One big honkin' thing," he will say with finality
later, from the safety of his trailer in the redwoods east of
Elk. "How's that for an estimate?"

I met Sinclair in the spring of 1995; I attended two of his
weekend seminars in ocean paddling and wrote two articles
about him; by ordinary measure, I did not know him well.
But when I returned home one evening recently to a
message that Sinclair had collapsed and died of a heart
attack at his shop on March 22, 1996, at the age of forty-
four, I was stunned. There was, of course, the shock of
youthful death, dismay for his wife Connie and their
three children: sons Ling, twelve, and Lloyd, ten, and
daughter Holly, eight, and the stubborn disbelief that The
Man Who Paddled in Hurricanes—a flesh and blood but
nonetheless mythical figure—was no more. Our heroes, to
some degree, become our property, and their disappear-
ances feel like personal affronts. There was, as well, the particular grief a writer feels at the death of a subject. For the
arguably mercenary purpose of his story, the writer affixes
his attention to his subject like a barnacle to a ship's hull

for a period of weeks or months until, and even after, the story is complete. Like an obsessive parent, the writer who is doing his job must interrogate his subject to a point just shy of harassment, must observe his every word and move. He must try, above all, to see the world through his subject's eyes. In turn, if all goes well, the subject grows to trust the writer—at the very least he grows to tolerate his scrutiny—and the two are bound together like laborers under the same foreman.

The youngest of five children, Sinclair was born in Claremont, California, in 1951. At his memorial service—the small church of Elk packed to standing capacity, 300 mourners spilling down the front stairs and out the back door into the church yard—his elder brother recalled a moment when their mother, exhausted by the tireless three-year-old, put Steve into a harness and staked him out in the backyard. I expected this anecdote to continue, their mother not realizing her mistake until the boy had pulled the property halfway across the neighboring county, but the facts themselves required no embellishment. At Claremont High School and Long Beach State University, he was an all-conference swimmer, lifeguard, surfer, and water polo player on the U.S. National Team. It was said that no one ever scored a point against him when he tended goal—there is a photograph of Sinclair rising like a kraken from the pool, bellowing, arms wide, eclipsing the net behind him—and I well believe it.

Gene McCarthy, Sinclair's high school swimming coach and lifelong mentor, introduced the twenty-year-old Sinclair to the Wave Ski in 1971. Designed by veteran surfer Merv Larson, the Wave Ski is a chop-tailed paddle-driven surfboard with foot straps and a shallow seat. Quickly mastering its talents in the surfline, Sinclair took the board to sea, chasing sailboats and freighters—and to the stupefaction of their crews, catching them—as far as fifteen miles from shore. Years later, off the coast of Elk, he once pursued and overtook the seventy-three-foot schooner *Varua* in his Odyssea ski. The ship was under full sail in a forty-mile-per-hour wind. Undetected in the heavy seas, Sinclair came up alongside to windward and roared, "Ship ahoy!" The startled captain fled belowdecks before remembering the helm; the two men later became friends.

In another incident, the twenty-four-year-old Sinclair and a friend entered a twenty-five-mile two-man rowing race from Catalina Island to Long Beach, in Southern California. At close to a quarter ton, their old practice dory far exceeded the minimum weight of 300 pounds required to enter. The other, more serious competitors had pared their vessels down to the ounce. A fourth of the way into the race Sinclair's companion suffered a hernia and abandoned his oars. With his partner inert in the 500-pound dory, Sinclair rowed on alone; hours later, they placed sixth out of more than twenty boats. As their bows thudded into the pier at the finish, the other competitors—all dedicated athletes—collapsed at their benches with exhaustion. Sinclair leapt out of his bow like Columbus, yelling for cold beer.

Merv Larson, in turn, introduced Sinclair to engineer and theologian Charles Sherburne, inventor of the Odyssea ski. Descended from the Australian surf ski of the 1890s, a craft designed for rescues in heavy surf, the wash-deck Odyssea ski was built for more than high performance in a gale. Fast enough to surf twenty-foot shorebreak, it is also a superb touring craft, carrying up to 300 pounds comfortably in forward and aft compartments.

Sinclair and his childhood sweetheart Connie Elwell, a skilled paddler and former competitive swimmer, married and moved to Elk in 1978. It was there, along the unforgiving Mendocino coast, that "storm sea skiing," as Sinclair called his sport of paddling oceanic storms, was born. Sinclair became Sherburne's test pilot, pushing the Odyssea ski to its limits, continually refining its design. He soon opened Force Ten, a paddling school and guide service in downtown Elk. On the calmer days of spring, summer, and fall, Connie Sinclair and the guides of Force Ten continue to lead tours in two-man kayaks (paddling experience not required) along the spectacular Mendocino coast. Meandering through sea caves like Dragon House, Saint Anthony's Elbow, and the Slot, parties pass abundant wildlife and beach for lunch on cliff-protected beaches accessible only from the sea.

Sinclair was as devoted a teacher as he was a practitioner

of his craft. Despite his fondness for winter storms, he was manic on issues of safety and frequently expressed his frustration at what he perceived to be a lax approach to water safety in the sea-kayaking industry at large. He was working on an instructional book, as well as a personal memoir, at the time of his death.

Sinclair argued that the vast majority of sea-kayaking schools fail to prepare students for the conditions they may face if they enter the ocean. The unwitting are trained on flat water and sold kayaks not suited to an open coast. This might be unobjectionable if inexpert paddlers never left the confines of a sheltered sound or bay. But neophytes are often released with the belief that they are sea-kayakers in the literal sense of the term. This is bad for the industry, worse for the souls who go out off a windless beach and find themselves caught in a howling aquatic inferno— with the wrong craft, the wrong experience, and the wrong skills.

During the opening lecture of a weekend seminar, Sinclair hammered and slashed at a blackboard with a nub of a chalk. He stressed ocean-kayaking as an in-water sport where complete immersion—in surf or building seas— must be prepared for. He considered even the warmest outdoor clothing—a common choice of many sea-kayakers—inappropriate, even unsafe, relying instead on a wetsuit. Sinclair preferred a wash-deck kayak, a boat you sit strapped to the top of rather than inside. In no danger of flooding, such a vessel—unlike a kayak with a cockpit—is as easy to right and remount as a surfboard. He insisted on a helmet regardless of conditions, citing the high ratio of deaths to injuries in water sports, where many drownings result from unconsciousness following a blow to the head.

While navigating an open coast, said Sinclair, always work to maximize your "down time." This is the time it would require, from any point along your course, to drift from the site of an accident, like a capsize or dropped paddle, into a potential hazard, like a wash rock or wave-battered cliff. With this in mind, attempt to pass rocks and other obstacles from the leeward (or downwind) side. To increase stability, avoid paddling a course parallel to the waves. If necessary, follow a zigzagging course, like a tacking sailboat, to keep the bow or stern near to the direction of the swells. Never take your eye from the sea.

Fundamentally, Sinclair's approach to handling open coastlines demanded a much greater degree of in-water skill than most sea-kayakers are led to believe they require. If you have any doubt at all about your water skills, he cautioned, start swimming laps. Unless undertaking a long open-water crossing, an endeavor which requires specialized training and equipment, never paddle farther from the shore than you can swim. Spend some hours in the shore break without your kayak, body surfing or Boogie boarding to apprehend the action of the waves. Sinclair argued convincingly that the advantages of being so prepared apply no less to the beginner in tame seas than to the storm sea skier in a gale.

Sinclair cited a conversation with a prominent sea-kayaking instructor at a San Francisco Bay Area kayak regatta. Sinclair had been stressing the importance of wetsuits and sound water skills to a gathering of newcomers. The instructor drew him aside. "What are you trying to do," he demanded, "raise the entry level?"

Outside Gunderson, Sinclair is in the trough, paddling skyward. He has been paddling since he left the shore and has not had time to buckle his seat belt. A dark shape looms suddenly from the depths of the face overhead. Sinclair rocks onto the port rudder and carves left, driving with his paddle. A sixty-foot tree with branches, roots, and a trunk with the girth of an armspan, breaches from the face of the swell and careens past him, grazing his stern. There is no shortage of such flotsam in a winter storm, discharged from Greenwood Creek, behind him, or from other estuaries to the north. Whole trees, logs, and the occasional telephone pole; some set like pikes in breaking faces, others rolling like mixers through the waves.

From the curling top of the swell, smaller waves of six or eight feet break off and sweep across the face in all directions. Some run over others and lend force. Others intersect at cross angles. They close like shears and break face-to-face, jetting a haystack of spray into the wind. Sinclair feints left and right, attacking these breakers with his bow. He works steadily uphill, crosses the swell's apex, and disappears completely in a veil of foam. Beneath the surface is the sound, as he puts it, of a hundred freight trains. He emerges from the foam and surfs down the back of the swell into the following trough. The next swell is rising, drawing him in. The sky vanishes. The attendant waves break off from the heights to intercept him. He streaks up the main face, gathering speed, evades the breakers, and launches from the summit of the swell into the air.

The boat rises, floats like a gull in the facing gale. Sinclair drifts from his seat and stands in his footwells. He leans forward, draws his paddle in line with the hull to prevent its blades from catching the wind and flipping him over. The swell passes beneath him as he falls. The boat finally lands, stern first, in the bottom of the following trough. He has lost time in the air and knows the next swell will break over him before he can attain its peak. He buckles his seat belt.

The top of the swell surrenders to the wind at its back and collapses like a cornice, roaring down the lower face in a thundering cloud of foam, inhaling the breakers in its path. Sinclair has faced similar conditions every winter for almost twenty years, yet the aspect of such an avalanche of sea bearing down upon him continues to inspire him with terror. He can only paddle.

Man and boat are struck and blown backward, in

Sinclair's words, "like a playing card thrown into a fan." The Odyssea ski tumbles end over end, whirling through the mass of raging sea. Sinclair holds his breath and lies flat against his back, clinging with both arms to the hull. He surfaces for an instant, sucks a breath, and vanishes again into the maelstrom of sea. The violence gradually ebbs. Finally Sinclair bobs to the surface in the foaming wake, back into the wind and rain. He turns his bow into the storm and paddles on.

As hour follows hour, the rhythm of the giant swells and the ceaseless wail of the wind begin to gnaw at the margins of his mind. He is suddenly struck by the fantastic absurdity of his position. He bellows incoherently, chokes with laughter. His mind yaws into a delirium which he will later compare to the prolonged conclusion of Kubrick's *2001*. It strikes him, with a jolt, that he is totally alone. Fear mounts and swallows him in a rush. He falls into his fear and soon wants nothing more than to let the paddle slip from his fingers, lower his head into his hands, and close his eyes. He will stop paddling and disappear beneath the surface of the waves. At the very bottom of his fear his mind grows quiet. He cannot hear the wind or feel the spray against his face. He feels nothing but a blessed warmth.

He continues to paddle. The fear has come before and it will pass. He begins to sing: Jimi Hendrix; *Electric Ladyland*. He paddles in long, steady strokes. The waves rise before him and he meets them with his bow.

Shortly before nightfall, Sinclair reappears at the mouth of Greenwood Cove. He surfs the twenty-foot shorebreak to the beach, carving up and out of the face and back over its shoulder before it closes out. From its position in the pocket, the Odyssea ski slings over the main body of the breaking wave and lands gently, high on the sand.

Sinclair lashes his boat to the rickshaw. When he is a quarter of the way up the hill, the Coast Guard helicopter passes overhead, its nose low into the wind. Sinclair waves, but they are already past him, their eyes on the darkening horizon. Notified by a passing motorist, they are looking for a solitary paddler, lost at sea.

For information on guided tours, call Force Ten in Elk, California: (707) 877-3505.

A Steve Sinclair Memorial Fund has been opened for the family at the Savings Bank of Mendocino, Box 687, Mendocino, California.

BENEATH THE ICE

It takes a saw with an eighteen-inch bar to get through the ice in the middle of the lake. When the chain reaches the water, it throws back a clear, arcing fount as thick as my thumb. I cut a triangle, six feet on a side. When I'm finished, I press down on a corner with my boot. It stands firm. I sink the saw back into the notch and take another inch, rocking the bar. Another shove with the heel. Now the slab rocks, water pushing up through the cracks and pooling along its perimeter. Two of us sink the floe with our weight and slip it to the side beneath the ice. On the black surface of the water, drops of oil twist into paisleys of electric green and plum. Beside them, upside down, float the summits of the High Sierra.

Over expedition-weight capilene underwear, a rag sweater, two pairs of wool socks, and a pile jumpsuit known as a Woolybear comes the dry suit. Coated nylon, airtight, it seals with rubber gaskets at the neck and wrists. Then the brass-ringed body harness, followed by the weight: twenty-five-odd pounds of lead shot in a nylon belt. Over this an inflatable vest, called a buoyancy compensator, then the tank, the regulator, neoprene mittens, hood, fins, and mask.

We clip lines into the rings on our harnesses. We tuck flashlights, secured by lanyards, into vest pockets, couple inflator hoses from our tanks to our dry suits, and turn on our air. We look at our gauges: tank pressure of 2,250 pounds; depth 0. My compass bevels freely in its chamber of oil.

Ice diving as a recreational sport is practiced wherever conditions allow, from frozen quarries in divers' home counties to the serpentine formations beneath the polar caps. Professionally, ice salvage divers make a fair sum winching trucks and snowmobiles out of lakes. Search and Rescue divers with the same skills save lives every year.

Aside from the support team of four, there are three of us waiting to dive. Greg is a carpenter, over forty, with hammer thumbs and trailing mustaches. He strikes one as a kind of mournful pirate. He drives a 1965 orange pickup held together by coat hangers and wads of electrical tape. The sadness that colors his movements on land seems to lessen when he nears the water.

Todd is a twenty-eight-year-old lineman for Pacific Gas & Electric. He gets up at four in the morning when storms throw townships into darkness, ripping poles out of the ground and releasing cables as thick as your forearm to writhe and crackle on the rain-washed blacktop. Sky diver, motorcyclist, one-time near-Olympic wrestler, he works his adrenal glands like bulldozer controls.

Todd and I prepare for the first dive. Bobbing in the water, we go over the signals with our line tenders. The slow bleed of adrenaline has sharpened the landscape. The low clouds tear their bellies on the peaks. We turn to the sun, gathering heat. Then we let the air out of our dry suits and descend.

In the first seconds, the unprotected skin around the mouth protests, then goes numb. We sink, watching for the bottom. At fifty feet the mud plain looms out of the darkness. We pump short blasts of air into our dry suits and arrest the descent, hovering, fin tips five feet from the bottom. Had we landed in the silt, or even brushed it directly with our fins, we would have sent a twin cloud of decaying organic matter in all directions. The pulses of current from our fin blades strike the membranous surface of the silt. Lace-thin, it quivers without tearing, like the coating of milk that has been boiled in a pan.

Far above the triangle is aglow in the dimly translucent field of ice. Our lines stretch upward, vanishing. I give a firm tug: "Okay." A tug comes back from my tender. "Acknowledged." The trail of air bubbles works its way to the surface, rumbling faintly. I take a deep breath and expel it with one quick contraction of the diaphragm. The body of air breaks into three spheres that flatten into mushrooms the diameter of dinner plates, expanding as they climb. Surrounded by a host of smaller bubbles—100 silver dollars, 1,000 dimes—twirling in their wake, the three upturned bowls of air catch the sun as they near the surface, gleam like mirrors, and disappear.

We send two tugs down the lines: "Going out, give us slack." Keeping our distance from the silt, we move across the bottom. We follow a bearing due north. If we become separated from our lines, a 180-degree turn should bring us within sight of the hole. A school of fingerling trout hangs motionless above a meadow of freshwater grass. We could pick them like apples, if we cared to, collect them in a bag. They're sleeping out the winter, drunk with cold. I touch one with a mitten tip. A tremor in the gills, the tail flickers once, then nothing.

Farther on is a dinghy, perfectly intact. Right side up, it floats becalmed on the surface of the silt. The benches and deck are evenly blanketed with pale sediment, as if abandoned on a winter beach, gathering snow. We sweep our lights beneath the benches, looking for a tackle box, an unopened bottle of beer. This wreck surrenders nothing— the work of other divers, or else a thorough abandonment of ship.

When we have used a third of our air, we ascend to the ice, still 500 lateral feet from the hole. We come up gradually, hands upraised to cushion the landing. Our breaths lie pinned against the ice in shimmering pools. Expanding with each exhalation, they elongate, break into beads. Following ravines and valleys too subtle for the eye, they seek the highest place.

The ice seems to glow from its core. Palpable as mist, it is a pale light in which no shadows fall. The ice is smoked through with minute bubbles. Cracks lost deep within it glitter like bayonets. I inflate the dry suit until buoyant enough to lie flat on my stomach against the ice. I push up onto my hands and knees and crawl a few feet upside down. With the heels of my fists I pound the ice. *Whump. Whump.* It's like beating the wall of a quarry. Our breath now forms vast sheets against the ice. When stuck, the ponds of air leap and scatter into beads of mercury, spiraling in the current of the blow.

Pushing off the ice, I stand upside down and join my partner. Hanging like bats, our exhalations tumble down our chests and break around our fins. There is a moment of vertigo before the inner ear accepts the artificial gravity of this inverted world, and then we're simply standing on the ice. The atmosphere above our heads is green, darkening to black. The luminescent plain at our feet is perfect and featureless as a glacier in the half-light of a gathering storm. The horizon is uniform, impenetrable. My hands are getting colder. I clench them into fists.

We check our air. It's time to head back to the hole. Turning south, we take the lines in hand and send a fast series of tugs. We brace, leaning back.

On the other side of the ice, our tenders set off like sled dogs at a run. The lines go taut and we begin to move, gaining speed. Howling through our regulators, we ski upside down across the ice.

The wedge of blue sky suddenly appears, hurtling toward us. As I dive headfirst through the triangle I'm blinded. I look straight down into the sun.

DARK PASSAGE

I drop to my belly in the grit and mud and slither beneath a fanged curtain of marble into a small chamber named the Dragon's Teeth Room in Lilburn Cave, deep beneath the ground in a Sierran canyon east of Fresno, California. When I regain my feet, Carol Vesely directs the conical glow of her headlamp toward the all but invisible aperture through which I just passed. "Take a good look at that," she says, "because on your way out you may not remember it." There are nine outlets leading in all directions from the chamber, many of them clearly apparent. But this cave, worn out of the marble by water trickling or rushing through its fissures for millennia, has hardly been designed for human use, and the appropriate exits are neither convenient, intuitive, nor marked. The low, emphatically uninviting feature that gives this room its name does not even resemble an egress: The navigable passage immediately behind the teeth rises steeply, for some feet, and appears to be a continuation of the chamber's irregular wall. But it is the only passage, from this region of the cave, that leads to the sun. I nod, forewarned, and secure the lithic maw to confident memory.

Vesely, now forty-one, is "the epitome of the gung ho woman caver in this country," according to caving historian Ernst Kastnings. She is right there with the best of the men. And she can outdo a lot of them." This sentiment is echoed by Dale Pate, a veteran caver and cave resource specialist for Carlsbad Caverns National Park. "One of the joys of going caving with Carol and other women like her is that they are *good*. Often better than me." In twenty-one years, Vesely has made 1,000 trips into 350 caves in fifteen countries, including the United States, Mexico, Austria, China, Papua New Guinea, and Belize. The chair of the National Speleological Society's survey and cartography section, she has surveyed more than 75 miles of underground passage worldwide. In 1986, with her husband Bill Farr, Vesely discovered Cueva Cheve in Mexico. Cheve is the second-deepest cave in the western hemisphere, 15.7 miles long and 4,547 feet deep at this writing.

Over this Memorial Day weekend, Vesely and sixteen other cavers have gathered at Lilburn to survey existing passage and push a number of the cave's remaining leads, or tributaries. If they're lucky, they will "scoop some booty"— or discover a virgin passage never before seen by man or woman. Years ago, some friends and I explored a wild cave in Colorado, and after one of our number became wedged in a squeeze and panicked and was finally freed, we stumbled upon a small subterranean lake shored by a perfect crescent of white sand. Since that time, I have visited a number of commercial and semiwild caves, in places like Oregon and South Dakota and Crete. Some of these were neon-lit and miserable and advertised on billboards on the sides of American highways, others were smaller but dark and undeveloped and beautiful. Virgin passage, however, is something I have never seen. And when the opportunity arose to join Vesely at Lilburn—these were some of the best cavers in the world, in the longest cave in California—I thought this just might be my chance. I gradually set my hopes, in fact, upon discovering a chamber—however small—and naming it for my infant daughter Julia.

At five feet four and 120 pounds, Vesely is slight and small-boned. Her blonde hair, worn long in a ponytail, is greying. She wears no makeup and broad-lensed eyeglasses and might strike you, in passing, as a schoolteacher or an academic. Until recently, she worked as a substitute teacher near her home in Monrovia, California, and she is just a dissertation shy of a Ph.D. in cognitive developmental psychology from the University of California at Santa Barbara. In addition to holding two part-time jobs, Vesely now works as a full-time mother. At the moment, her two-year-old son Brian awaits her on the surface, in the company of his father, at a rebuilt miner's cabin minutes from the cave's north entrance. A laser designer, electrical engineer, and computer scientist, Bill Farr is a speleophile with an extreme if not morbid fondness for cave diving, or scuba diving in subterranean waters.

One of the first (if not the very first) things one learns from cavers is that they categorically do not care for the term "spelunker." A spelunker, I gather, is anyone who wanders ill-advisedly into a cave without adequate equipment or training. Not even young Brian Farr is a spelunker; he has already accompanied his parents into fifteen caves.

As an undergraduate, Vesely dabbled broadly in outdoor sports, including skiing, white water rafting, skydiving, hang gliding, and rock climbing. She wanted to try them all, but stayed with caving. "From the very start," she says, "I loved the idea of going somewhere no one had gone before. On one of my first caving trips, the guy who led it pointed at a hole and said, 'I don't think anyone has ever gone through there.' I jumped right in. Who knew what would lie beyond?"

Our team of four includes Vesely, Roger Mortimer, Art

Fortini, and myself. Mortimer, thirty-three, is a physician in family practice and AIDS consultant from Fresno, California. Since 1984, he has caved in the United States, Canada, France, Austria, and Malaysia. Fortini is a thirty-five-year-old chemical engineer from Pasadena, California. A mountaineer and alpine Search and Rescue volunteer, he has been caving for thirteen years, in Belize and across the United States. At five foot six and 130 pounds, Fortini appears ideally proportioned for subterranean travel. Stripped to his long johns, the wiry, Bronx-born caver looks very nearly capable of entering a house through the cat door.

We aim to investigate several potential leads in an area of the cave known as the Schreiber Complex. One of the leads is marked cryptically on the map: "Hard climb—Roger knows the way." Not this Roger; the note was scrawled several years ago by an unknown hand, and Mortimer has no recollection of the climb. Our group is temporarily accompanied by computer security expert Bill Frantz and archaeologist Maryanne Russo. Russo, forty-five, has fifteen years of caving experience. Frantz, fifty-three, has been caving for nearly thirty years. Frantz is particularly familiar with this area of the cave and will guide us to a turnoff close to the high climb. At nearly sixteen miles of known passage to date, with much that remains unexplored, Lilburn is the longest cave in California. The vertical distance from the highest of two entrances to the cave's deepest point is 510 feet.

A caver's standard equipment includes boots, durable

and preferably waterproof coveralls and gloves, a helmet, an electric or carbide headlamp, spare batteries or carbide, no fewer than two reserve light sources, and a small pack containing food, water, a first-aid kit, and extra layers of clothing. Many cavers also wear knee pads, and in a cold cave like Lilburn, a hat, or balaclava, and one or more layers of synthetic long underwear. In warmer caves (the temperature in some caves in Mexico hovers at more than 100 degrees Fahrenheit), cavers may strip to their shorts or skin. Not only more comfortable, this also decreases the cavers' cumulative, inevitably destructive impact on delicate surfaces and formations. For technical sections involving climbing or rappelling, cavers carry harnesses, static caving rope, and climbing hardware. Cave divers must haul scuba gear, usually in stages, from the mouth of the cave to the dive site—commonly a sump, or submerged passage.

We follow wordlessly in single file, ducking and crawling and slithering, scooting and sliding on our heels and backsides, climbing and crabbing over boulders big as cottages, shimmying through chimneys, skirting chasms, passing blades of marble sharp as guillotines. The marble is speckled or striped or swirled in every conceivable pattern of black and white and blue-grey. The patterns are wild and artful, as apparently random as the forms and hollows themselves, which endlessly constrict and broaden, arcing and twisting, rising and climbing and dropping away into darkness. The cave is cool, at forty-six degrees, and damp. The stone sweats; water pools in low places. The nether reaches of the cave flood periodically, and a sediment of granitic sand often chokes the floor—where floor exists—of the passageways. In places, the marble is concealed, spackled by the ebbing torrent with a coat of fine sand that brushes off under a glove.

Ahead, Russo slips. We are traveling unroped, exposing ourselves to falls to a degree that we might not tolerate, as Mortimer later observes, under the all-revealing light of day. In the selective glow of my headlamp, a yawning ravine to the right—its shadowed depths chaotic with cracked blocks, lunging tusks, and broad, gently curving sails of marble—is less intimidating the moment I direct my gaze upon the narrow, sandy shoulder of marble that traverses it. Abandoned to darkness, such features cease in a sense to exist. At the moment, happily, we are only stemming along a narrow fissure, walking with each foot on opposing sides of the crack. When Russo soundlessly missteps, she wedges her leg to the knee—but no more. Vesely helps Russo to her feet and we continue. Ahead, the others' headlamps bob and broaden, softening as they sweep up and across wide passages to illuminate the walls, then tight again, condensing into brighter pools at their feet or dazzling pricks of light upon their hands.

My plastic-coated gloves soon become slick and coarse with mud—ooze penetrates the elastic cuffs and a fine, grainy fluid like iced Turkish coffee trickles down my forearms to the elbows and into the tips of my gloves. In places, water drips unexpectedly from above into the collar of my overalls.

We soon arrive at the Great White Pillar, a forty-foot column of gleaming ivory calcite, or flowstone, in a small chamber fifteen minutes from the cave's south entrance. Frantz, Vesely, and others have made frequent trips into Lilburn to clean and repair such formations, muddied or damaged over the years by accident or intent. The need for such active conservation has increased apace with rising traffic through Lilburn and other caves worldwide. We pause to admire the formation, then part ways with Frantz and Russo. My group of four continues toward the Schreiber Complex, eager to investigate the climbing lead. We discover that the climb has been choked by a cave-in, called "breakdown" by cavers. Wherever that passage led—at least from this direction—is sealed forever. This is not uncommon; breakdown is the last phase of a cave's natural life cycle. The trick, I reflect as I contemplate the densely packed jumble of mud and marble blocks, is to make sure you're not around when it happens. While Vesely studies the map, Mortimer and Fortini make short reconnaissance trips into neighboring passages. Vesely is unsure if a narrow chimney nearby has been explored, and I clamber up it, shinnying with elbows and knees. It is a slender corkscrew of slippery mud, marble, and rippled orange flowstone, and it ends shortly in a tight passage clogged with sand.

We break for lunch at the union of a deep crack—black as pitch, impenetrable to the headlamp, and wide enough to admit a careless body—and a sandy crawlway. There is no room left in the sand and I seat myself comfortably on a large chockstone wedged in the fissure. On either side of my bench lies the abyss. I drop a small pebble on each side. Tic . . . tic-ack . . . tic . . . tic . . . tac . . . tic . . . and on they tumble out of earshot. I dine on bagels and energy bars, but Fortini has been more resourceful. He produces a cheese pizza, kept warm against his ribs in his cave pack.

The sandy passage has already been scooped, or previously explored, but remains unsurveyed. After lunch the cavers produce compass, inclinometer, measuring tape, and sketchbook. Fortini will lead, crawling ahead with the tip, or "dumb end," of the tape. I will manage the reel, or the tape's "smart end," and read the numbers to Vesely, who will sketch the passage and record data. Mine is the task best suited to one, like myself, with no surveying experience. Mortimer will shoot compass bearings and inclinations, and Fortini will shoot back-sights to confirm Mortimer's accuracy. Fortini crawls ahead and selects a prominent feature, called a "station," at the farthest line of sight from the station last established on the map. This may be anywhere from a few feet—most common in a mazey cave like Lilburn—to many meters in distance. Lilburn is measured in feet, and for mathematical ease the tape is marked not in inches but in tenths of feet. "On station," says Fortini, six or seven feet from my position. He shines a small lamp on his station for Mortimer to take his shots. "Tension," I say, and Fortini holds firm as I draw up the slack in the tape. "Seven point four feet," I tell Vesely. Mortimer peers into his compass and reads the bearing. Then he takes up the inclinometer—both devices can fit together in a breast pocket—and reads the inclination: "Six degrees positive." Vesely notes these figures, then returns to her sketch of the passage. In places she makes cross sections in addition to vertical outlines. I illuminate my station and Fortini shoots back-sights. In this case, they uphold Mortimer's readings, and we proceed. Unlike traveling through the cave, which is steady and athletic, surveying is slow, careful work, and by the third station, twisted on my back in a tight crawlway, I realize just how wet and chilled and filthy I have become. Surveying gives you time to think—at least when you're running the reel—and when you're wedged in a cold slot underground, time to ponder is not always a good thing.

"I ask myself if I would do this voluntarily," I say aloud. "The surveying, that is. And I suspect I wouldn't." Vesely snickers from somewhere in the wobbling gloom. "You couldn't pay most cavers enough to do any of this," she says. "But they'll do it for free. Wouldn't you agree, Roger?"

"The finished map," says Mortimer after a pause, "is an object of beauty."

The passage zigs and zags and zigs again, and soon I have an opportunity to enjoy another of the cave surveyor's myriad pleasures. I am standing in eight inches of sucking mud, and I cannot read the tape because it, too, is mud-covered. I streak it with a muddy thumb, back and forth, with no result.

"Lick it," advises Fortini, and I do so. The mud is cool, grainy, and absolutely without flavor. But the tape is clean.

After more than an hour, we reconnect to a previously surveyed passage, stow the instruments, and meander on. I have actually warmed to the process, by that time—eating another bagel and donning a second layer of capilene in the interim has helped—and feel some regret, surprisingly, that there is no remaining passage in this area of Lilburn to survey. We soon emerge on the rocky shores of a small lake. The water is still, shallow, and perfectly clear. We follow a climb that skirts the lake and at one point I drop left and down alone into a three-by-three-foot windowed chamber that offers out across the lake like an opera box.

When we turn for the surface, Mortimer bows slightly in my direction and gestures down the passage. "After you," he says. I choose correctly at a handful of the major unions. But when we enter the Dragon's Teeth Room—despite Vesely's explicit warning—I fail to recall it, so jumbled are Lilburn's countless turnings in my mind. I glance tentatively up and into three of the most obvious outlets and overlook the teeth entirely; they lie in one dim corner, all but brushing the floor. The others wait silently behind me. "I think it's this way," I say finally, obeying my intuition, and start up a climbing passage in the wrong direction.

I make a few additional errors, each politely corrected, before we finally emerge into a pale night sky. The smell of the woods is astonishingly pungent and sweet. It is nine-fifteen; we've been underground for more than eight hours. After several days in a cave, Vesely tells me, one grows accustomed to the color (it is yellow but appears white) of artificial light. When one emerges finally into daylight, the greens and blues of jungle or forest and sky are wondrous, almost hallucinatory, as if the eyes had never before encountered those hues. The ears are startled by birds.

A short hike down the trail, the shingled, one-room cabin stands amid sequoias and cedars and ponderosa pines on the canyon floor. The cabin's windows are shuttered, its roof sharply peaked. At more than 1,500 meters above sea level, the night air in May is still crisp, and smoke trails from the stone chimney. Within the cabin are voices; a glimmer of yellow light escapes along the frame of the front door.

Cavers crowd the room, gathered in a semicircle on crude benches and folding aluminum chairs. A broad stone fireplace faces the door. A bottle of brandy stands uncorked on a table. In one corner is a wood stove; military storage lockers line the opposing wall. A wooden ladder climbs through an open trap to a sleeping loft. Grey, dusty coils of stiff rope, steel cable ladders, small, battered packs, paired boots, helmets, neoprene wetsuits, oil lanterns, and a body board—a strapped sled with which to immobilize and haul an injured caver—hang from countless hooks on the beams. The ceiling is low enough that a person of middling height brushes against many of these items while navigating the room. These tired objects, in browns and greens and duns, impregnated with dried mud, appear strictly utilitarian and antique; even at second glance one might suspect their owners to be nineteenth-century miners, or veterans of the Somme. On the long mantelpiece is a rusted climbing piton, a jar of calcium carbide, a bottle of lens defogger, a pile of widowed gloves, a medical text, a harmonica, the jawbone of a deer, a Rubick's cube, a Dorothy Sayers mystery, and a million-dollar bundle of Joss money. The $10,000 notes, imprinted with a portrait of Confucius, are typically burned at Taoist weddings for good luck. At an Asian market in the United States, the exchange rate is about one American dollar to a million joss. Among cavers, I'm told, the notes are handy for lighting cigars.

Over the weekend, seventeen cavers—some accompanied by their families or noncaving friends—pass through the cabin. At eleven o'clock in the evening, you cannot move in the small room without elbowing a Ph.D. in the ribs. There are geology professors, chemists, aerospace engineers, schoolteachers, computer programmers (including a Russian caver with a doctorate in Artificial Intelligence), a doctor, an archaeologist, an economist, a biologist, an electrician, and—a token student of the humanities—an information scientist (or postmodern librarian) at Berkeley. The mean I.Q. among this scruffy, mud-smeared band of pit crawlers, I imagine, must hover somewhere over 150.

"We're all misfits," says Farr, a book entitled *Radiation and Noise in Quantum Electronics* open in his lap.

"As a girl," says Vesely, "I was exceptionally shy. I was uncomfortable in crowds. I was a social outsider. I don't think I know any cavers who were ever in the 'in-crowd.' A lot of cavers, when they finally find caving, feel that they finally fit in. I can go anywhere in the world, and all I have to do is find another caver—not even someone I know. I'll call them up and tell them, 'I'm a caver from California,' and they'll invite me to their house and let me camp on their floor. And I do the same thing."

The cavers in the cabin drink brandy and ouzo and wine—from the bottles or from camping cups—and some step outside to smoke cigars. To the accompaniment of guitar and harmonica, some sing obscene or scatological ditties and limericks. The most presentable of these involves "a couple named Kelly, who went around belly to belly, because in their haste they used library paste, instead of petroleum jelly." I might overstep the bounds of journalistic decency to recount also the tale of "a man from Racine, who invented a frigging machine. 'Twas concave or convex, and would suit either sex, but it sure was a devil to clean." They pore over the multicolored map of Lilburn tacked to the door—there are rooms and passages with names like Impossible Dream, Thanksgiving Hall, South Seas, Mousetrack, Mud Heaven, the Penthouse, and Bloody Way—and tell stories of caves across the known world.

Farr recounts a cave dive in which he clawed upstream through a passage so narrow that he had to remove his tank and push it ahead of him, into a current nearly powerful enough to tear his mask off. Farr describes this experience as "relaxing."

Brian falls asleep in Vesely's lap. Before his birth, Vesely spent three months a year on expedition, averaging fifty or sixty trips annually. As a mother, these figures have been cut in half. "It's well worth the trade-off," she says. "Having a child is like finding virgin cave every day. You never know what's going to happen. You go through a miserable, scuzzy little crawlway and the next day you find a beautiful new chamber." As a mother, she claims to have lost some of her boldness underground; given the difficulty of extracting victims through tight, labyrinthine passageways, even minor injuries in caves can prove disastrous. "I hope that passes," she says.

When Brian was eleven months old, Vesely joined an expedition linking two lava tubes on the island of Hawaii, creating the longest cave—at twenty miles—in the United States. Thirteen miles into the trip, as prearranged, Vesely left her fellow cavers at an underground campsite, crawled from a side entrance, and drove to a hotel where her mother-in-law waited with Brian. Vesely spent the night with the baby and sped back to the underground camp in time for breakfast.

I ask Vesely if she has encountered any sexism in a sport long dominated by men. "It's come a long way," she says after a diplomatic pause. "There used to be a lot more. But twenty years is a long time. When you're younger, especially as a woman caver, it takes longer to get accepted, and there's a tendency for people to want to help you. Men automatically want to be chivalrous, and give you a hand on a climb, or take your pack. And unless you assertively say 'No thank you,' it will happen to you, and there are some women who figure, 'Well, they're offering, and that's no problem,' and go along with that—but I think it can hold you back."

The following morning the cavers rise slowly. There is an unwritten tradition, enforced by brandy, that cavers should never leave camp for the cave before noon. Vesely informed me of this the previous morning, as we left the cabin at eleven fifty-nine.

Half a dozen cavers, including Vesely, spend several hours burrowing in a pair of congested sinkholes north of the cabin. These sinks, they believe, may one day open into the mythic but reasonably postulated Great North Cave, a twin to Lilburn suggested by water action on the surface. If the Great North Cave is eventually exposed and linked with known passageways, the total area of navigable cave may double or treble Lilburn's current dimensions. Later in the afternoon, Vesely and I join Jeff Cheraz and Mark Scott for a trip into Lilburn via the north, or Meyer, entrance. Cheraz, a thirty-year-old electrician from the area of Pasadena, California, has been caving since the age of twelve. The twenty-six-year-old Scott is a British doctoral student in aerospace engineering at Stanford. He has been caving for eight years.

Standing near the entrance—a padlocked gate set into the hillside and invisible from the trail below—we and our helmets are perceived by a pair of male hikers. The men pause and peer up through the trees.

"Are you guys cavers?" one inquires. There is a long, uncomfortable silence. No one in the caving party moves.

"Is that a cave up there?" the man presses.

"We're not at liberty to say," says Cheraz and tries to smile.

The hikers finally move along. Cavers are infamous for this sort of behavior toward outsiders, in part because non-cavers going into caves too often require a rescue—a grueling undertaking in the best of circumstances, and often dangerous to the rescuers involved. There is a bumper sticker which reads SPELUNKERS ARE RESCUED BY CAVERS. Most important, they say, cavers attempt to thwart noncavers' access to wild caves because underground environments are so extraordinarily fragile. Of all wilderness areas, caves are by far the easiest to damage and the most difficult, if not impossible, to repair. "People don't realize that one careless moment can destroy a formation hundreds or thousands of years in the making," says Vesely.

The irony that cavers themselves, as careful as they may be, inevitably damage the cave is not lost on them. "One of the first things I learned was the paradox of caving," Dale

Pate later tells me. "The cave is pristine until you as the first person discover it. After that, it's changed irrevocably. It's a huge responsibility."

"The best caver I have ever seen," says Vesely, referring to the late Phillipe Rouiller of Switzerland, "moved through a cave as if he were floating."

Ducking through the Meyer entrance, the four of us descend a forty-foot vertical pit via cable ladder. While standing at the base of the pit, waiting for the last person to descend, I nearly step backward into a bowl of cave pearls—spheres of calcite formed around grains of sand by decades of gentle agitation in shallow, stream-fed pools. "Watch it!" says Scott, pointing, and I catch myself. But I have very nearly been the case in point.

We inspect a series of potential climbing leads without success—bootprints in the sand betray that these passages, while unsurveyed, have already been scooped. Later, returning to the surface by another route, a slender crack in the shape of a horseshoe descends between a bulge of marble and the wall. Vesely leads, feetfirst, and as her head slips into the finest part of the crack, her helmet catches. She shifts her position slightly, the helmet scrapes through, and she disappears from sight. "Clear," she calls, after a moment, and I start down. Resting my pack atop the bulge, I slip my boots, legs, and hips easily into the crack. With my arms gripping the slope, my toes pawing gently for small ledges, I slide deeper into the crack and stop short, stuck in the squeeze. I exhale and slide deeper, but not deep enough. With a sharp thrust of the diaphragm, I expel the last breath from my lungs and push again. I inch still tighter and stop. The pressure against my back and chest is not painful but unyielding, and I cannot breathe. In the near-darkness, underground, I am pinned by my own doing between two unyielding immensities of stone, incapable of drawing a breath, my legs dangling invisibly, my arms stretched out across the sloping marble. It is fortunate that I am more afraid of open spaces than of tight places. In any case, I can descend no farther. I reach out with my toes, grope for footholds, find them, push myself up and out of the crack, and take a breath. I try again, more circumspectly, and find that if I lean slightly farther to the right, I can slip my torso comfortably through the constriction. I slither downward and emerge beside Vesely in a lower passage. "A squeeze is like a combination lock," she tells me. "You only need to know the combination."

At caving conventions aboveground, cavers often squirrel themselves through adjustable wooden "squeeze boxes" in good-natured competitions. In the safety of this controlled setting, cavers may push their capacities far beyond what they might hazard underground; for the convention's remainder they may wear pins declaring their tightest squeezes, measured to the eighth of an inch. For an adult of normal weight, the size of one's narrowest possible squeeze usually approximates the full span of their hand, from thumb to little finger. In men, the broadest part of the anatomy is usually the upper torso. A woman is most commonly arrested by the depth—front to back—of her pelvis. A very slender woman's tightest squeeze may be defined by the width of her skull turned sideways. Some women thus emerge from squeeze boxes, triumphant, with mirrored abrasions over their cheekbones. At parties, improvising, some cavers will pass through wire coat hangers bent into rings. I have attempted this unsuccessfully in the privacy of my living room and can report that it is a good deal more difficult than it sounds. Bill Frantz once brought a squeeze box to a junior high school class, and the two smallest girls in the class attained the tightest squeezes. "They were the best at something physical for once," says Frantz, "and they were thrilled."

In the end, we scoop no booty in Lilburn. Julia's Room is out there, but it remains buried, perhaps in another cave, on another continent.

On our way out, still deep underground, our party pauses in a domed chamber floored with sand. I lay my pack against the wall, stretch out in the cool sand, and rest my helmeted head comfortably against the pack. I turn off my headlamp. During the weekend, I have observed cavers who at odd moments did likewise. They laid their heads upon their packs, extinguished their lights, and closed their eyes, sometimes with their arms curled up beneath them, their cheeks upon their hands. One minute here, two minutes there, the cavers catnapped while others studied the map, took a drink of water, or changed the batteries in their headlamps, and they looked as comfortable, perched on a flat slab or stretch of sand, as if they were in their own beds. Now, Scott joins me, propping his pack against the opposing wall. Vesely and Cheraz disappear down adjacent passages, reconnoitering. The wavering of their lights and the sounds of their footsteps grow fainter and fainter and finally vanish. The blackness is absolute. There is no sound but a distant, resonant dripping. My eyes are useless in the colorless void, and after staring at the darkness for a while, I close them. Scott lies motionless nearby. I breathe and listen to the drip of the cave. Minutes pass. My limbs sink into the sand. After a time, I can no longer feel the empty hollow of the chamber around me. I feel nothing but the sensation of incalculable depth, and the deliciously protective, all-concealing weight of the darkness, hard as stone.

For more information on caving or local caving groups, please contact the National Speleological Society at (205) 852–1300.

THE PRECIPITOUS WORLD OF DAN OSMAN

At dawn on his thirty-second birthday, rock climber Dan Osman breaks the world record, his own, for a free fall from a standing structure. Using nothing more than the modified equipment of his trade, including single climbing ropes, a full body harness, and a reinforced anchor, he jumps an estimated 660 feet from a bridge in Northern California. The bridge soars some 700 feet above a wild river valley.

During a safety meeting in the hours before departure for the bridge, tasks are relegated to the members of Osman's support team—in this case, fellow climbers Geoff Maliska, twenty-three, Osman's unspoken disciple, and Anthony Meeks, twenty. Precise details of the protocol and rigging are reviewed. Upon arrival at the site, they move out across the girders of the bridge, beneath the traffic, 700 feet from the valley floor. Osman rigs the elaborate anchor—a nest of nylon loops, or runners, climbing rope, and aluminum hardware—near the middle of the bridge. Leaving Meeks to watch the anchor in the capacity of downrigger, Osman continues with Maliska another 160 feet across the span.

The greatest danger in a fall of such a distance, Osman believes, is not the failure of the system, which is sound, but entanglement within the rope. The force of impact achieved at terminal velocity, he suspects, could bisect or decapitate a body wound in the 10.5-millimeter rope.

To be certain he can extricate himself from such entanglement should it ever accidentally occur, Osman will intentionally wrap himself in the rope as he falls. He will uncoil himself and assume the correct position within the seven seconds before impact. The attempt is unprecedented.

When he nears the launching point, the rope hanging slack beneath the bridge in a huge arc, Osman ties in. Originating at this lateral distance from the anchor, much of the fall's inertia will be diverted upon impact into a rocketing swing 500 feet across the valley floor. As opposed to falling directly from the anchor position, this decreases the chance of entanglement and keeps initial impact forces—a striking whip when the rope runs out of slack—within reasonable limits.

Osman checks his harness and knots three times, examines his clothing for anything that might affect his fall. He looks down the rope, signals Meeks. Meeks checks the anchor, returns the signal—all is clear.

Osman begins to scale a girder, gaining the height necessary to break the record of his previous fall. The beating of his heart becomes unmanageable and he stops. He clings, closes his eyes, and fights for air, tries to breathe deeply, to slow his heart, to dilute the load of adrenaline. Electric shocks fire like needles in the muscles of his hands, arms, and legs. Breathing, breathing, Osman beats back his fear and continues up the girder. He does this twice, each time climbing farther before the panic mounts again and overwhelms him.

He reaches his launching point and stops. He closes his eyes.

Three minutes later he opens his eyes and looks out across the valley. It is dawn. Passing cars drum intermittently overhead. There are fishermen in the river, far below. He watches the movement of their rods. Their voices rise faintly.

He closes his eyes again and visualizes the entire sequence of his fall, dilating the seven seconds into eleven or twelve. He will execute three cartwheels. In the middle of his third cartwheel, he will twist his body and in so doing wrap himself one full turn in the rope. He will then unwrap—calmly, methodically, he will not thrash, he will not thrash—and extend his limbs, relaxing as he enters the point of impact. It is only when he completes the visualization that the risk of what he is about to attempt becomes clear. In the wake of this realization, his fear leaps to the next plateau. Sweat bursts from his pores and freezes. Goose bumps swarm across his skin and explode into flame.

He glances over his shoulder at Maliska, signs thumbs-up. Maliska is struck by the horror in Osman's medusan gaze, but he grins and returns the affirmative gesture. "Happy sailing," he calls.

Osman looks out across the valley. He steps through what he calls the moment of choice. From fifteen Osman counts down silently, breathing, saying only the ten and the five aloud. Four, three, two, one. And then he falls.

To climb at the edge of your ability is to fall, and the equipment is designed to keep those falls from causing injury or death. But the equipment, on occasion, fails, and the climber fails more often than that. On rope or off, it is the fear of an unchecked fall—a bone-snapping, skull-crushing fall—which nags most climbers, holds them back, thwarts their inspiration.

In 1989, while ferreting from virgin rock the line of Phantom Lord—a route of his creation—lunging for uncertain holds, Osman fell. Over and over. And like any climber with imagination, he feared every fall for the unthinkable. He began to realize, then, that it was not in climbing but in falling that he would embrace his fear, bathe in it, as he says, and move beyond it. So he began to fall on purpose, from greater and greater heights. Osman's comfort and performance on the rock has improved accordingly.

As a boy in Rockland County, New York, I spent many unwise hours climbing with cohorts on Hook Mountain. The Hook is a geological appendage of the Palisades, which rise like a curtain along the western bank of the Hudson River north of the George Washington Bridge. We climbed with little more in the way of equipment than canvas basketball shoes, cut-offs, and Yankee caps, and the degenerate rock came out in fistfuls like rotten teeth as we ascended.

We continued north on bikes along the river, past Haverstraw to the Bear Mountain Bridge. We skidded down the steep embankment from the road to walk across the girders underneath the bridge. We trotted, then jogged back and forth across the grey-green rivet-studded beams, each one a foot, perhaps fifteen inches wide. We leaned slightly into gusts of wind to keep our balance, several hundred feet above the rocks along the river's eastern shore.

In the twelve or fourteen years that intervene, I have only dabbled in the media of ice and rock. I have traversed glaciers in the North Cascades, climbed in the Rockies and Shawangunks, bouldered in Fontainebleau and Joshua Tree.

I am tied to the hills, but I know them—by Osman's standards—only vaguely. Beside the likes of Osman, I am not even a climber. In the cheerfully unminced words of Geoff Maliska, I am a flatlander.

This path not taken brought me to Lake Tahoe, California, to meet Dan Osman, to watch him climb and fall. For psychological self-improvement and lust for adrenaline are inadequate reasons to explain what might propel a sane and careful individual like Osman to hurl himself from cliffs and bridges, risking all. To begin to understand the drive to fall, one must try to understand the drive to climb.

I stand at the base of a decomposing granite outcropping south of Lake Tahoe known as the Pie Shop. A rope lies loosely gathered on the flat top of an adjacent boulder called Lunch Rock. Unwinding from its center, the rope follows the ravine between two stones, rises through the shivering branches of a manzanita bush, and moves vertically across the granite face. Eight point eight millimeters in diameter, the rope is diamondbacked in fluorescent orange, yellow, and green. The accumulated friction of its passage produces an amplified hiss in the windless silence that ebbs and swells in rhythm with the progress of the climber above.

Despite the rope attached to his harness, Osman is free-soloing the 165-foot climb. There is no belay. He places no protection. He is merely carrying the rope to the top for a later, more difficult climb, and any fall will send him to the earth. Osman is lithe, under six feet. His dark hair, long enough to cover his shoulder blades, is bound in a ponytail. In the 1890s, Osman's paternal great-grandfather, a descendent of samurai families in the Takeuchi clan, emigrated to Hawaii from the mountainous Iwakuni region of Japan. Takeuchi was killed in 1910 on a sugar plantation in the act of disarming a fellow laborer who was preparing to assassinate their foreman with a revolver. As a boy, Osman was trained in the samurai ethic of bushido by his father, Les Osman, a twenty-one-year veteran police officer. The young Osman studied aikido, and later, kung fu.

Climbers speak often of elegance—elegance of climbing style, of route. And it is undeniable that climbing without rope is more elegant than climbing roped, as climbing roped but mechanically unaided is more elegant than gadgeting skyward with ascenders and rope ladders, called etriers. The catch of free-soloing, and its appeal, is the simplicity of the equation it demands: One cannot fall. Like the kendo practitioner who lays aside his wooden sword to duel in earnest with live blades, the climber—in freeing him or herself of the rope on routes where falling is synonymous with extinction—becomes a kind of mystic.

In preparation for a difficult solo, Osman will climb the route several times on rope, repeating the crux, or most difficult move, until he is certain he can execute the climb without error.

"Then I start breathing," he explains, "to get the *ki* down into my hara." Loosely translated from the Japanese as "vital energy," *ki* is not an abstraction but a tangible phenomenon, as significant to the martial artist as harmony to the musician. The *hara* (literally, "belly"), a point in the abdomen below the navel, is held to be the center and source of physical energy. It serves as a reservoir of sorts, in which *ki*, largely through breath control, may be pooled and from which it may be directed.

"I visualize a screen," Osman continues, "a steel filter which I lower with my breaths to keep the positive energy and let the negative energy escape." When he is centered—a process which takes fifteen or twenty minutes—he is ready to climb. "I feel the air pressure. . . . The *ki* is very concentrated, very strong. . . . I feel the gravity more. When I step onto the rock . . . my senses immediately sharpen. The taste in my mouth becomes vivid."

Despite the ease of this route for a climber of his ability, Osman appears to spare nothing. His pace is unhurried. The expression on his face is a void. Even on large, so-called positive holds, the placements of his hands and feet—the latter tightly shod in pale blue, red-laced, black-soled rock shoes— are unerringly precise. Without interrupting the liquid flow of his movement, he seems to consider each hold as if preparing to catch the raised head of an asp. When he makes his placement, it is final. There is no shuffle, no grope. For all of his fluidity, there is an awesome mechanical beat to his progress. *Bang. Bang. Bang. Bang.* He seems to climb within a field generated by the concentration of his will, a shimmer which moves with him and eludes the eye.

The route is *Earn Your Wings*, 5.9a. Climbs are rated according to a numeric class system devised by the Sierra Club Mountaineers in the 1930s. From Class 1, walking, through scrambling at Class 2, the rating mounts to difficult free climbing (mechanically protected but unaided) at Class 5, and concludes with aid climbing (mechanically assisted in resting and ascent) at Class 6. Class 5 is subdivided through the addition of decimals. These are further nuanced by a plus or minus (e.g., 5.8+) or even more precisely with a letter, *a* through *d*. the distinction between a 5.12d and a 5.13a is often subtle enough to be practically indistinguishable, and sometimes a matter of debate. The difference of a full decimal point, however, is substantial; dedicated climbers can spend months or even years advancing from 5.10 to 5.11, from 5.11 to 5.12. The most difficult free climb in the world as of this writing—infamous for its dynamic, one-finger moves—is *Action Directe*, 5.14d, in Germany, placed by the late Wolfgang Güllich.

With the encouragement of his mother, Sharon Louise Burks, a horse trainer and two-time world champion barrel racer (a rodeo event involving agile horses, standing barrels, and figure eights), Osman began climbing at age twelve. Despite his evident talent, he describes himself as a slow developer, taking eight years to break through to 5.12.

Completing *Earn Your Wings*, Osman proceeds to solo a

short piece of his own design: *Funky Cold Medina*, 5.10a, an overhanging corner above 160 feet of air.

A difficult route can take months for a climber to establish, or "place." The completed route is christened and rated by its author. Subsequent climbers will confirm or challenge the rating—climbs are often downrated as climbers work out easier sequences over time—and soon the route will appear, immortalized, in local climbing guides.

Osman takes immense care in the creation of his routes, his greatest satisfaction praise from other climbers for the spare beauty of his "lines." He regards each climb as a monument, not only to its creator but to the climbers of generations past who attempted the route unsuccessfully—with equal boldness but inferior technology—as well as to those who follow and attempt the route. The spirits of these climbers, Osman believes, past and future, will remain imprinted through their efforts on the rock.

From *Funky Cold Medina*, Osman continues to another of his offspring, *Buttons of Gold*, 5.9+, named for the tawny nipples of rock which serve as holds. He then moves through the boulders which crown the broad-backed outcropping, executes short, powerful sequences on overhangs an arm's length from the ground, leaps from stone to stone.

Carrying the coiled rope over his shoulder, Osman crosses to the eastern prow of the outcropping, stepping lightly in his rock shoes over beards of crusted snow. He drops down into a notch and emerges beneath and to the side of a swollen bulge of granite that droops over the vertical face like an enormous collapsing soufflé. A horizontal crack, centimeters to inches in width, runs 40 feet along the joint between the bulge and the face and curves obliquely to disappear. From this crack, an unchecked faller would travel 280 feet to the ground, glancing once upon a sloping ledge midway.

Osman anchors the rope, ties in, and whitens both sides of his hands with powdered gymnastic chalk from a pouch at his waist. The chalk marginally protects the hands and keeps them dry of sweat.

The climb is *Blood in My Chalk Bag*, 5.11 c/d. Osman's belayer is Meeks. Anchored through his harness to a boulder, Meeks feeds the rope through a belaying device that will help him brace a potential fall. Osman is said to be "leading," because he will place protection at intervals along the route as he proceeds.

Osman moves out across the section of the face between the belay ledge and the overhang. He pulls himself into a hemispherical notch in the outside of the bulge and rests on his heels, rechalks his hands. He grimaces faintly, nagged by three recently broken ribs (snowboard, tree), and stretches his torso. He slowly releases a breath, then drops out of the notch and begins the climb.

The footholds on the nearly vertical face below the crack are thin. Most of Osman's weight, in a technique known as smearing, is supported by the friction of his soles against the texture of the granite. He carefully jams his left hand deep into the crack. With his right, he unclips a Friend—a spring-loaded camming device—from a loop on his harness. Holding the device like a depressed syringe, he inserts the retracted head into a section of the crack best suited to its width. When he releases the trigger the opposing cams, or curved wedges, expand and seize the rock with metal teeth. He tests the piece with a tug, clips his rope into the carabiner that dangles from the Friend by a nylon loop and continues. The carabiner is an oblong ring of aluminum alloy about the length of your palm and equipped with a spring-loaded gate. A semantic cousin of Mussolini's enduring *carabiniere*, the carabiner, ubiquitous in climbing, was originally invented to clip carbine rifles to bandoleers and may still serve that function. A climbing carabiner's minimum breaking strength in the direction of its long axis is 2,000 kilograms, or about 4,400 pounds.

While still well below the limit of Osman's ability, *Blood in My Chalk Bag* is a workhorse. In contrast to the day's first solo, Osman's execution here is simian, dynamic, a display of tenacity and brute strength. Dispelled by vigor is the shimmering haze. Some of his positions appear awkward, out of balance, but he is climbing as the route demands. With his right hand and right foot jammed into the crack, Osman pauses briefly, hangs to rest, slackens his opposing limbs. Soon he vanishes around the bulge and finishes the climb.

Meeks, whom Osman has known for less than a week,

decides to follow, cleaning the route of its protection as he goes. Osman will belay. Meeks is soon in trouble. While skilled on faces, his crack technique is no match for the route. His progress is painstaking. Osman encourages, coaches move by move. The light fails in the snow-dusted valley below. The temperature drops. A Friend resists extraction. Meeks wrestles with the recalcitrant piece, swears at it, finally falls. He hangs on the protection and rests. The darkness deepens. Placing another device beside it to relieve his weight, Meeks finally gets the Friend out and continues. He finishes the climb and appears on the crest of the bulge, stands silhouetted in the dying sky.

Osman is not his teacher, but the role is unavoidable given the discrepancy in age and skill. It is also a role which comes naturally, aided by the almost beatific humility which informs his every word and move. Coiling the rope, he praises Meeks's tenacity but gently reprimands him for not being entirely honest with himself or with Osman, given the route, his skill, the time and conditions. Meeks nods, abashed. In the silence that follows, he holds out his hands as if examining a manicure, looks thoughtfully at the blood-spotted chalk on his knuckles, and smiles with pride.

The following morning Osman and company appear out of the mist at Cave Rock. The Cave, as it is known, is an ominous and nobly situated vault—like one half of a cathedral's dome—hewn by erosion from the cliffside far above the fog-swept eastern shoreline of Lake Tahoe.

Despite the single lane of highway that passes not far below its base, it is the kind of cave, were it to be found in the Aegean, in which Olympian divinities were rumored to be born.

The floor of the cave, once punctuated with condom wrappers, disposable diapers, and shards of green and amber glass, is now a lithic garden. With help, Osman devoted more than 300 hours to the construction of belay benches, gravel pathways and quietly decorative stone formations. The result approaches a monastic courtyard.

Osman steps from the gravel floor onto the wall of the cave. With the delicacy of a watchmaker and the strength of a longshoreman, he rises up and out across the increasingly inverted roof. The route he follows is *Phantom Lord*, 5.13c. While he has crafted more technically demanding climbs, like the neighboring *Slayer* at 5.13d—a route praised by Wolfgang Güllich as the most elegant he ever climbed—none rival *Phantom Lord* for boldness.

Arriving at the end of the seventy-foot overhang, Osman climbs over the lip to the anchors. He has finished the climb and for a moment rests. He calls down to Maliska, his belayer. Then he falls.

His body careens out away from the cliff and plummets earthward, limbs flung wide. Maliska, like Meeks before him, is secured to the rope through a belaying device. The force of the fall travels to the belayer through the fulcrum of the anchor overhead. At the moment of Osman's impact on the rope, Maliska leaps from the ground in the direction of the pull.

This ultradynamic belay is essential lest the faller arc too soon and too abruptly from the fulcrum overhead. A static or inflexible belay would rob Osman of the necessary slack and catapult him in and up against the cavern's jagged roof. He would strike the rock at a speed approaching sixty miles an hour. This potentially fatal error has already been made, by another belayer who leaned back instinctively to brace a similar but accidental fall. The resulting impact broke both of Osman's ankles.

Osman falls sixty-five vertical feet, completing two cartwheels, and swings gracefully into the lower recesses of the cave. Maliska, plucked cooperatively into the air by the force of Osman's fall, hangs from his belay, legs braced against the wall twelve feet above the gravel floor.

In the process of perfecting such a fall, Osman has done more than grapple with his fears. By greatly exaggerating the conditions of normal climbing falls, he has in five years gathered enough data to potentially revolutionize the technology and application of climbing protection. He is currently designing or modifying equipment, including protection and belaying devices, as well as developing techniques—including body positioning before and during impact on the rope—to greatly improve the safety of long climbing falls.

But there are costs. In May of last year, Bobby Tarver, a

twenty-five-year-old bungee jumper in Osman's circle of close friends, was killed replicating one of Osman's falls. Unable to accompany Tarver to the site, Osman first attempted to forestall him, then precisely outlined and diagrammed the preparation of the fall. Tarver was impatient. "You could see it in his eyes," says Osman. "He was looking at the paper, but he wasn't listening." Tarver proceeded to a bridge that spans a Utah canyon, failed to execute a simple preliminary step, and fell 250 feet to strike the canyon wall. He regained consciousness briefly and died three hours later.

Osman has returned to that bridge on three occasions since the accident, twice to jump. Both times he retreated from the edge. He now plans to descend into the canyon, speak with Tarver. He will then remount the bridge. Choosing to ignore technical refinements made since the tragedy, he will jump precisely according to the plan he diagrammed that morning in May.

At the time of my visit, Osman lives alone in a warm, sepulchral studio 200 yards from the shore of Lake Tahoe. The bed, couch, chair, and table in the main room abut like puzzle pieces. Along one wall stands a work bench layered with climbing hardware: camming devices, chocks, carabiners, ice axes, snowshoes, crampons, a red helmet. A coiled rope lies yoked over a vice. Propped against an electric guitar amplifier is a red and yellow backpack, a prototype of Osman's design for the North Face, a prominent equipment manufacturer. Two snowboards lean in the corner by the door. There is a small television, an ample collection of rock-climbing videos. Seven or eight books stand on a bedside table, each of them concerned with Japanese history and the samurai, including an epic novel on the life of Miyamoto Musashi, Clavel's *Shogun* and *The Samurai Sword: A Handbook*. Photographs of Osman's daughter Emma, age eight, are visible from every angle in the apartment. On the walls are posters, a balance of heavy metal bands—notably Metallica—and climbers on varying terrain. Twice appearing is Lynn Hill, a ground-breaking climber now working at the top of her form. Osman cites Hill, together with the current mentor Jay Smith, Wolfgang Güllich, and legendary soloist John Bachar (pronounced "Backer") as exemplars.

From beneath his bed Osman reverently withdraws a Japanese long sword, or katana, its curved scabbard sheathed in blackened shark skin. The sword's hilt is veneered with the dimpled ivory skin of a stingray, bound in a lattice of burnt-orange silk. The wave-tempered blade is nicked and smudged in places by irreparable corrosion. The sword has certainly seen use.

Returning from the Pacific with an American serviceman, the sword came into the hands of Les Osman at the cost of a bartered shotgun. Experts have since confirmed the weapon's age in excess of 400 years. Reserving it for this occasion, the elder Osman presented the katana to his son in an informal ceremony last Thanksgiving. Considering himself undeserving, the younger Osman unsuccessfully attempted to decline.

"He had earned the right to have possession of the sword," Les Osman, once skeptical of his son's vocation, now recalls. "Doing the work that I do I have faced death many, many, many times. When it's over, you celebrate the fact that you're alive, you celebrate the fact that you have a family, you celebrate the fact that you can breathe. Everything, for a few instants, seems sweeter, brighter, louder. And I think this young man has reached a point where . . . his awareness of life and living are far beyond what I could ever achieve."

On the day of my scheduled fall, I wake at four in the morning in the excessive heat of a motel room in Stateline, California, and see Tarver hanging from the rope in the middle of the Utah canyon.

Hours later, I remain uncommitted as I stand at the edge of the overhanging cliff across the road from Cave Rock, far above the boulders that lie like Galápagos tortoises in eight inches of water on the shore of Lake Tahoe. I am attached to the anchor, to the cliff, by a slender hanging arc of nylon.

Earlier, in the car, I had suggested the possibility of a second rope, a backup, should one fail.

"You could do that," Osman answered. He reflected,

seemed to weigh his words. "But . . . that's not really what it's about."

He seemed to object to my suggestion not in judgment of my cowardice, which his expression seemed to say was my affair, but in defense of ritual. As if, because he knows a second rope to be superfluous, the aesthetic and thus the spirit of my jump would be defiled.

A layer of mist hangs like a belt above the western shore, bisecting the snow-covered peaks that rise beyond. The lake is vast, an inland sea.

Osman points. "Do you see the rock that looks like a skull?" The large stone is pale, ninety-five feet directly below, the sockets and mouth implied by dark patches of lichen. "That is your landing zone," he says. "Step off and aim for that rock." "Whatever you do," he continues, "don't jump out. Don't jump out. Don't jump out. If you do, you may swing into the cliff."

I ask Osman to check the anchor. I have been married less than a year and I doubt the wisdom of this. I question my motive. I question the technology involved. For some reason, I do not question Osman. He climbs up, checks the anchor, returns. I feel impelled to thank him, shake his hand. I continue to breathe. I stand facing the anchor, farther south along the cliff, the outside of my right foot flush with the edge of the precipice.

In a mutation so swift as to be imperceptible, as if externally compelled, I pass irreversibly through Osman's moment of choice. In the attenuated heartbeats that fall between the moment of commitment and the moment of execution, the pooling fear distills, climaxes, and transmutes. The resistance of the will cracks like a misshapen endoskeleton and dissolves. The body, suddenly unbound, becomes weightless, soars in its position on the rock. The back straightens, the head instinctually rises to the sky. A deep, luxurious passivity imbues the limbs. The oxygen is rich, heavy, pulled in long, even draughts. I have gained no deeper confidence in the equipment. I have in no way lost the visceral suspicion that I may soon lie mangled on the rocks below. I have simply been relieved of my command.

I count to three and step off the cliff. The sensation of the fall begins at once, without the anticipated poise in space. The shoreline within range of my peripheral vision vaults skyward. The cliffside smears into a blur. The acceleration exceeds all expectation. No dream fall, no gently arcing adolescent cannonball from a high board has prepared me for the rate of my descent. I am not falling. I have been hurled—spiked, perhaps—with celestial gusto from the sky. I lock my eyes on the skull between my feet. There is a last spasm of panic, a final lashing of the dormant will. I release a long, shapeless cry.

The free fall lasts little longer than two seconds, a mere 35 to 40 feet before the slack is out. The tension on the harness pulls me gently from my course, directs me south into a long swing of 200 feet, parallel to the overhanging cliff. I shout obscenely. The sky is full of angels. My hands tremble as I lower myself, still swinging, to the shore. I finally alight and stand, freeing the rope of my weight. Dan Osman calls triumphantly from high upon the cliff. I accepted his temptation. I leapt from the precipice and was upheld.

In expanded form, this story appears in *Fall of the Phantom Lord*, a book about climber Dan Osman. Osman was killed by equipment failure in a roped fall three months after the book's publication. A trust fund has been established for his daughter Emma: The Emma Osman Trust Fund, 1760 Roper Court, Reno, NV 89506.

STILLWATER

On the rocky coast of Sonoma County, California, beyond a
row of police and park vehicles in the small lot at Stillwater
Cove, a white helicopter trimmed with silver and burgundy
rests on the beach. It is ten-fifteen in the morning on
Saturday, April 1, the opening day of abalone season.

Randy Riggins, a thirty-one-year-old abalone diver, lies
flat on his back on the sand. His eyes and mouth are open,
his head is tilted back. His skin is waxen. There is thick sa-
liva on his lips and cheeks. A tube uncoils from a needle in a

vein inside his elbow and rises to a bag of clear liquid held aloft by a park ranger.

Lloyd Noble, a paramedic with the Sonoma sheriff's helicopter unit, lies on his stomach in a wetsuit and inserts a plastic tube into the diver's throat. He is trying to establish an airway. Roger Rude, the sergeant in charge of the helicopter unit, prepares to give the diver air. Deputy Bob Pacheco, the helicopter's observer, kneels beside Noble and pumps fluid from the diver's lungs into a plastic reservoir. Produced by the tissues of the lungs after contact with salt water, the pint of fluid in the container is foamy, the color of straw. Sergeant Dave Nagle kneels at the diver's side and performs chest compressions: slightly more than one per second. He rocks from the hip, silently counting, his weight against the heels of his palms.

I crouch in a position where I can see the diver's face. My heart drums. There are grains of sand and beaded water on his skin. His hair is short, his cheeks unshaven.

Noble can't establish the airway. There is too much fluid; the tissues are hopelessly inflamed. The compressions are making his heart work, but Riggins is not getting air. Without oxygen, the darkening blood that moves through his limbs is worthless.

Ten feet to the south, Riggins's partner Larry Anderson kneels in the sand. The hood of his blue wetsuit is pulled back. His gloved hands hang at his sides. His back is straight, his body absolutely rigid. His expression is stunned, vacant, but in his fixed, unblinking eyes there is wildness. It is the expression of a man—physically composed but unresolved—before a firing squad. If there is energy in that cove, an energy like heat, it emanates not from the swift and rational actions of the rescuers but from the figure of that diver on his knees.

Riggins coughs, foam spraying from his mouth. My heart skips. I wait for him to gasp, to cough again, to groan. But it was only fluid, forced from his chest by the compressions.

I finally back away, circle to the south, and stand a short distance behind Anderson. He hasn't moved, as far as I can tell, since I arrived. After a moment I come up beside him, lean down, touch his shoulder, and ask if he wants to come out of the sun.

He doesn't turn his head. "I don't want to leave him," he says.

On last year's opening day, while thirteen-foot swells hammered the rocky cliffs and coves around Salt Point, the helicopter unit pulled five divers from the water before noon. In the same period, State Parks lifeguards, using inflatable boats and surfboards, hauled out five more.

"We get a tremendous amount of people from the Sacramento valley," explains helicopter pilot Dave Boyce, age forty-eight. "They don't get a chance to see the ocean very often. They've been thinking about this for months and months and months. They pick up their family, they pack up their bags, they get out here, and it's like 'Look at that. Look at those waves.' And his wife is saying, 'Don't be stupid, the waves look terrible,' and his buddy's saying, 'Have another brewski, man, we're goin'.' So he slams down a couple more brewskies, and out comes the courage, and into the water they go."

State Parks lifeguard Don Straub has pulled nearly fifty abalone divers out of the water every year since his arrival at Salt Point in 1990. In many cases, Straub explains, accidents happen when beginners follow more experienced partners into conditions well beyond their abilities. Others neglect the buddy system entirely. "They're partners until they reach the water's edge," says Straub. "After that they're pretty much on their own." While free-diving instruction is available, no certification is required for abalone divers. Straub is not alone in his desire to see this change. While many divers would balk at such a proposal, there's no doubt that mandatory instruction in the basics of ocean reading and water skills would prevent a great number of diving accidents on the Northern California coast.

Although hundreds of divers are rescued by the helicopter unit and the lifeguards every year, twelve abalone divers have drowned in Sonoma County since 1985. In most of these cases, seas were reported as rough or hazardous, with swells ranging from four to eleven feet. One twenty-seven-year-old diver was overweight and thought to have no experience in the ocean. He overexerted on the hike to the beach, say witnesses, then ignored warnings from a rescue diver not to go out in rough conditions. Seen out of breath and spitting water on the surface shortly after making his entry, the victim was separated from his partner by a set of waves and drowned. His blood alcohol level at the time of his death was .15 percent—nearly twice the legal driving limit in California. Another twenty-seven-year-old was dashed repeatedly against the rocks and drowned. No test for drugs or alcohol was performed. If the man was clean, he may have had almost everything—youth, experience, and good health—in his favor, except the judgment required not to dive in poor conditions. Faced by the waves, two of his three companions decided to remain ashore.

Cousin to the snail, the whelk, and the sea slug, the abalone is a single-shelled mollusk found in kelp beds worldwide, including species off New Zealand, Australia, South Africa, and the Pacific coast from Baja to Alaska. Equipped with a powerful gripping muscle, or foot, abalone graze on drifting scraps of kelp and hide in rocky crevices from sea otters, bat rays, and other predators. Their empty shells can often be seen gleaming like mother-of-pearl on the kelp forest floor.

Cut into steaks or strips, softened with a club or studded abalone hammer, then barbecued, broiled, or fried, abalone meat has an unexpectedly sweet and earthy flavor. Scoma's Restaurant in San Francisco offers a seven-ounce abalone steak for $54.95. The restaurant buys the meat directly from a commercial diver—"Deep Diving Frank"—for $58.95 a pound. Small wonder that recreational divers suit up and go after the gastropods themselves. One seven-inch abalone— the minimum legal size—can provide two pounds of edible meat. Multiplied by four—the recreational diver's daily limit—this comes to a feast worth nearly $500 wholesale.

Thanks largely to heavy commercial harvesting on the California coast—5 million pounds a year at its peak in 1957—a sharp decline of the local abalone population has forced a law forbidding the use of scuba for recreational abalone diving in Northern California. Equipped with a mask and snorkel, wetsuit, weight belt and fins, the abalone diver requires a fishing license, a flat-handled bar called an abalone iron with which to lever, or "pop," the muscular shellfish from the rocks, and a measuring gauge with which to confirm the abalones' legal size. Divers are advised to work in pairs, trailing a float, or covered inner tube, in which to secure their game. Using a system known as leapfrogging, one dives while the other rests on the surface. If the diver down fails to ascend, his partner can dive to his aid or summon help from shore. Most divers work at depths from fifteen to twenty-five feet, with average bottom times of under thirty seconds. For the inexperienced, it may take several dives to find and secure an abalone. Masters can reach depths of seventy feet, with bottom times of a minute and a half or more. A skilled diver in an abundant area can often surface with his limit of four from a single dive.

Near dusk on Friday, March 31, the helicopter rests in the grass on a bluff in Salt Point State Park, overlooking the Pacific a few miles north of Stillwater Cove.

Dave Boyce stands at the edge of the bluff and considers the horizon. The ocean, uncharacteristically, is calm. Boyce flew helicopters for fourteen months during the Vietnam War, inserting SEALs and Special Forces into contested areas of Indochina.

Sonoma, a rural county of apple orchards, vineyards and dairy farms, lies an hour north of San Francisco. Its fifty-three-mile coastline—a ragged hem of cliffs and rocky coves—is notoriously unforgiving. Pounding seas, strong currents, and a chilling average water temperature of fifty degrees kill a handful of divers, boaters, and beachcombers every year. Last winter, along the neighboring coast of Mendocino County to the north, a woman's family gathered to scatter her ashes at the site of her drowning. A rogue wave struck the party of mourners in the midst of the ceremony. The victim's daughter was swept to sea and also drowned.

Beyond the helicopter, sheltered by a stand of pines, the sheriff's helicopter unit lies camped with a trained force of approximately seventy-five Search and Rescue volunteers. A few rescuers have brought their families. Small children rattle back and forth in plastic cars, rear-ending each other with shouts. Picnic tables are laden with potato salad, venison, and barbecued chicken. The atmosphere is festive, muted only faintly by the prospect of impending action.

To the south, near cliffs that drop abruptly into narrow, rocky coves, the public campsites gradually fill. Hundreds of divers pitch their tents, check their gear, and celebrate the best opening day forecast in years: three-foot swells and fifteen to twenty-five feet water visibility.

By seven the following morning, the wind is picking up. The sky is pale, cloudless but for a streak of white on the horizon. It is opening day, and eight- to ten-foot swells roll in from the northwest and crash on the headlands. So much for the forecast.

Frances Focha, a firefighter with the San Francisco Fire Department and a Sonoma County Search and Rescue volunteer, stands at the edge of the bluff and watches four divers move along the shore through her binoculars. The divers wear black wetsuits and carry floats over their shoulders, their multicolored fins in their hands. They're looking for an entry through the line of rocks. From a distance, over their backs, their circular floats look like the shields—one hot pink, another neon green and orange—of a warrior tribe. The divers pause, watch a wave hit the rocks with an explosion of spray, and continue on.

Dressed in orange jumpsuits and equipped with walkie-talkies, Focha and the other volunteers will observe hundreds of divers from positions along the coast. At the first sign of a diver in trouble, they will radio a dispatcher in the mobile command post: a trailer parked below the bluff at North Gerstle Cove. Within moments, the helicopter will be in the air.

A 4,150-pound light-utility aircraft, the Bell Long Ranger III has an operating ceiling of 20,000 feet, a maximum airspeed of 150 miles per hour, and a price tag of $1.1 million new. It flies with a crew of three: pilot, paramedic, and observer. The observer serves as navigator, provides a second pair of eyes for the pilot, and assists with rescues.

With an annual budget under $50 million, Sonoma is not a wealthy county. The sheriff's department considers itself fortunate to have a single, three-man helicopter with which to perform all air-based law enforcement, medical evacuation, and rescue operations—an average of 900 missions, or details, every year. Of these 900 some 150 will be rescues, frequently of divers, stranded climbers, and the victims of Sonoma's all-too-common floods. For rescues performed during the flooding of Sonoma's Russian River in 1986, the crew was chosen from hundreds nominated internationally for one of the industry's highest honors: the Crew of the Year Award for 1987 from Helicopter Association International.

At the heart of the unit's capability is the long-line rescue system. Long-lining is the transportation of a load attached to the helicopter's belly hook with a rope or cable. There is no hoist involved. During a rescue, the pilot moves the rescuer and victim like a pair of fishing weights on the end of a leader. Adapted, in Sonoma's case, from commercial applications, the long-line system has saved close to 100 lives since its adoption in Sonoma in the early 1980s.

Roger Rude describes a typical rescue of an abalone diver in distress: Arriving at the scene, the pilot circles the victim briefly while assessing the conditions, then sets down at a suitable landing zone, or LZ, on shore. While the observer and the paramedic prepare the rope system—a 100-foot static climbing rope attached to the helicopter's cargo hook—the pilot removes his door to increase his field of vision. The paramedic and observer decide between them who will perform the rescue.

"We always have a rescuer involved," Rude explains. "Victims are poor candidates for self-rescue. You can't lower them a rope or a rescue device and expect them to know what to do with it."

Already wearing a wetsuit and climbing harness, the rescuer pulls on a pair of fins and clips into a locking carabiner, or aluminum alloy snap link, on the end of a Y near the rope's end. Attached to the other end of the Y is a horse collar—a padded loop which will pass beneath the victim's arms. At the rescuer's signal, the pilot lifts the rescuer from the LZ and carries him to the victim. The third crew member remains at the LZ and prepares to offer medical treatment. Leaning slightly out of his open door, maintaining direct sight of his cargo, the pilot lowers the rescuer into the water. The pilot hovers briefly in position while the rescuer secures the victim in the horse collar. At another signal, the pilot lifts rescuer and victim out of the water and returns them to the landing zone.

"The whole scenario," says Rude, "from arrival at the scene to the time we can effect the rescue, will take from two to seven minutes." These are not rehearsals, he points out; these are live.

Like the hydraulic hoist, the long-line system permits rescues in environments where the helicopter cannot land. Long-lining also dramatically reduces hovering time—a drawback standard to most hoist operations. Comparable, Rude explains, to balancing on a beach ball, hovering demands a particularly high degree of pilot concentration. Requiring as much as 50 percent more power than forward flight, hovering also greatly increases the strain on the aircraft. "And if the engine quits in a hundred-foot hover," says lead pilot and fellow Vietnam veteran Tom McConnel, "you'll go down like a piano."

Perhaps the greatest advantage of the long-line system is that it enables a single, light-utility helicopter—the airborne equivalent of a modestly priced 4X4—to safely effect rescues at speeds equaling or exceeding those performed by larger, hoist-equipped helicopters far outside the budget of most rural counties.

I drive down to the mobile command post and take a ride with State Park ranger Ashford Wood, following a dirt road along the cliffs to the neighboring cove of South Gerstle. We stand on a headland near two Search and Rescue observers and count the half-dozen divers in the cove. The sun-dazzled surface of the water churns with foam. Between descents, catching their breath, the divers cling to their floats, rising and falling with the swells that roll through the cove between the cliffs and break on a crescent beach of stones the size of basketballs.

Wood walks north along the cliffs between the coves and spots three divers, clambering through tide pools to a rocky point. Outside the cove and unsheltered, the point is battered by waves. Wood scrambles within earshot.

"Have you guys ever dived this spot?" he shouts. The divers nod.

"Do you know about the rip currents?" Apparently they do.

Wood asks them to be careful—he can't stop them—and we head back to the truck.

Over an hour later, two of these divers are spotted on the surface at the mouth of North Gerstle. One of them, apparently fatigued, is receiving a tow from the other. There's no need yet for the helicopter, but the divers aren't far from the rocks on the south side of the cove, and the swells are edging them in that direction. A lifeguard decides to go after them.

Wearing a wetsuit and a kayaking helmet, he paddles out on a surfboard. The divers accept a tow to shore, and Wood is there to greet them. "Remember me?" he asks. The divers nod sheepishly, denying fatigue.

"We were just messing around," one claims. "Going slow."

They are brothers, in their early twenties. Neither of them have any abalone.

At two minutes after ten a call comes in from Stillwater Cove to the south. There are reports of a diver, apparently unconscious, on the surface. The crew scrambles. The helicopter lifts into the air.

On Friday evening, after working a full day as a frame carpenter, thirty-one-year-old Randy Riggins played catcher, first base, and right field in a baseball game with a city league near his hometown of Antioch, California. After the game, Riggins and his wife Christine joined friends for dinner. Over darts, Riggins complained of sore legs to a friend. By six the next morning, when Riggins left for Salt Point with fellow carpenter Larry Anderson, an abalone diver with twenty years of experience, he'd had less than four hours of sleep. Christine Riggins was up before he left, feeding their infant son Gary, age six weeks. She noticed the wind outside their inland home and asked her husband not to dive. Riggins cheerfully shrugged off her concern and told her he'd be back by noon.

After taking an abalone diving class four years before, Riggins had been diving steadily once or twice a month throughout each season. He lifted weights three or four days a week. Except for a sore lower back—the cost of his trade—he was in good shape.

On the drive north, the two men stopped for gas and coffee. Anderson had called the coastal conditions hotline—a service offered by Salt Point State Park—the night before and again at four-thirty on Saturday morning. The forecast remained fair. The divers didn't know that the hotline is updated daily at 7:30 A.M. Anderson heard Friday's forecast twice.

They arrived at Stillwater Cove shortly before eight o'clock. The seas, of course, were not what they expected. Anderson described conditions at the time as "lumpy," but there was no discussion of canceling the dive. They geared up and entered the water shortly after nine. Riggins was using borrowed fins: a stiffer pair than he was used to. By nine forty-five, having made four or five dives in water no deeper than thirty feet, Riggins had secured one abalone, Anderson two. Then a large wave broke over Anderson as he rested on the surface. He looked back at the sea. "In half an hour," Anderson said later, "conditions had gone from divable to what the hell are we doing here."

They immediately turned for shore. Faced by a stiff tidal current as they kicked back into Stillwater Cove, both divers had to work to gain ground. Thirty yards from the beach, another big wave rolled through. The two men were tumbled and separated. Anderson regained his bearings, kicked the short distance to shore, and caught his breath.

A bystander called down from the cliffside; she had seen the wave hit, she told Anderson, and could see his buddy in the middle of the cove, resting on his back on the surface. Anderson thanked her and walked up to the road in his wetsuit. By the time he brought the truck down to the parking lot, he figured, Riggins would be out of the water.

Minutes later, other witnesses on the cliff directed diver Rocky Daniels—paddling alone in a sea kayak—to the motionless diver. Riggins, floating on his back, had pulled his mask and snorkel down around his neck, a standard practice that prevents their loss. A panicking diver will usually remove his mask entirely or push it up onto his forehead. From a distance, Daniels said, "I wanted to believe he was resting. But when I got within ten or fifteen feet, I could tell he was in trouble." Riggins's eyes and mouth were open, but he showed no response to the surface chop that washed across his face. He had ditched his weight belt; a sign that he had known he was in danger. By the time Anderson pulled into the small lot at Stillwater Cove, several other divers in a zodiac were rushing the unconscious Riggins to shore.

The rescuers prepare to move Riggins up the beach into the helicopter. A park ranger cuts the diver's new wetsuit—

a Christmas gift from his wife—away from his arms with a pair of blunt-tipped medical scissors. On a count the rescuers pick him up and slide the stretcher beneath him, then move swiftly as a unit to the aircraft's open door.

Anderson breaks his stance as they load Riggins into the helicopter. He bends over, rests his elbows on his thighs, and lowers his face into his upturned hands. His forehead almost touches the sand. He holds this position while the helicopter turbines sing to life. The heavy whoofing of the main rotor and the high whir of the tail rotor fill the cove. The sand sprays up from the beach and Anderson stands, confused, crouching in the buffeting wash of the helicopter. He sees his buddy's gear strewn on the beach near the water and lurches forward, scrambling, gathering it in against his chest before retreating up the beach with the others.

It takes the helicopter fourteen minutes—an hour and a half trip by land ambulance—to reach Palm Drive, the closest hospital. Despite continued efforts to revive him, Randy Riggins is pronounced dead at 11:05.

Larry Anderson drives back to Antioch alone, a pile of empty clothes at his side.

Autopsy confirmed that Riggins had not been drinking. He had suffered no other apparent injury, and the cause of his death was established as salt water drowning. How, one wonders, can an experienced and healthy diver die so quickly on the surface? I spoke later with Dr. Allen Dekelboum, a diving medicine specialist in San Francisco. Struck by as little as a couple of drops of water, he explained, the larynx can spasm and seal the trachea, or windpipe. While preventing the entry of water into the lungs, this defensive mechanism also deprives the victim of air in an experience akin to choking. This can lead to unconsciousness in what is called "dry-drowning." The victim's larynx will usually relax upon loss of consciousness, triggering a reflexive breath and, if submerged, admitting water into the lungs. In a less likely scenario, Riggins may have suffered what is known as sudden death syndrome. In rare cases, divers with no known heart condition have suffered fatal heart attacks, usually on the surface. Such attacks seem to result from overexertion and the particular stresses placed upon the circulatory system by diving.

Three weeks after the accident, Roger Rude and Lloyd Noble catch up on paperwork between calls in the hangar outside Santa Rosa. Dave Boyce stretches out on a sofa. Noble describes the detached frame of mind, called "flat affect," that paramedics and other rescuers maintain during an attempt to save a life. "I'm just processing information," he explains. Disassociation may be necessary at the moment of performance, but earlier in the day Noble appeared distracted and subdued. He muttered, jokingly, about the need to find some other line of work. He said he had recently asked his son, an abalone diver, to dive farther north, out of his call area. Finally he turned slightly from his desk to Roger Rude.

"I've been thinking about my ghosts, Roger," he said with a vague smile.

"Your ghosts?" answered Rude.

"I see too many faces," Noble said.

A wooden cross now hangs in a tree overlooking Stillwater Cove. It was hung there by Christine Riggins, two months after the accident. I had visited their home in Antioch a month before. I met their children: Taryn, age five, and Gary, then three months. Randy's blue truck was in the driveway. His brown dog was in the yard.

I spoke with Christine Riggins again after her visit to the coast. "It's getting harder," she admitted. "It's just been so long since we've seen him."

"I know it wasn't his fault," she said, referring to Larry Anderson. "It happened so fast. I don't think he could have done anything, even if he'd been with him. I just don't understand how he left him." She didn't say it with malice. Just confusion, and regret.

"I can't say we really did anything wrong," Anderson tells me a month after the accident. "But I felt guilty. I drove us up there. I led him out, I led him in. We were diving my spot." Anderson says he's been waking up with nightmares. "Randy just had a son," he continues. "I mean, God, cut it out." He pauses. "Why not me?" he says. "I wanted it to be me."

As a scuba diver, I often pause in sandy clearings in the kelp. Hovering on my back near the bottom, I relax completely. My limbs hang weightless. I watch the sun break through the canopy above in knives of amber. I listen to the crackling of the fish and the rumble of my exhalations rising. In all directions, the swaying strands of kelp recede into near-darkness. My breaths create a widening hole in the canopy until a sixty-foot column of unbroken sun illuminates the glade like a chapel. Schools of small fish gather in the sun. The forest and the fish and I swing gently as one body in the surge. I make no motion until my air begins to dwindle.

In the ocean I have made my share of bad decisions. Most I made consciously, negligent of risk. I was raised in the ocean, I would argue. Its rage would punish, I believed, it would instruct, but it would spare my life. I acted upon this belief until it brought me so close to the truth that I began to evolve, in stages, into caution. Nearing thirty, I feel the gratitude of one awakening from madness. But in part I mourn this transformation. And in spasms I contest it, I still push, because the wisdom of timidity reeks so powerfully of death.

Beyond the vanished life of Randy Riggins recede wakes, invisible to me, of disbelief and heartbreak and some sense, I imagine, of injustice. His children will grow into these emotions as they age, until the bitterness and sorrow, too, appear to vanish, like fence wire lost in the heart of an old tree.

THE WRECK
OF THE BELLE

Twelve feet beneath the wind-ruffed surface of Matagorda Bay in Texas, seventy-five miles northeast of Corpus Christi on the Gulf of Mexico, the silted bottom dissolves between my groping fingers like the finest, silken dust struck by a broom. The three-inch visibility drops to zero. The ambient light diminishes; pale mustard-green darkens into rust. I raise my console to within a finger's width of my faceplate, strain to read the depth and pressure gauges, and discern nothing but a lump of shadow.

The water is warm; there is no appreciable current. The only sound is the hydraulic hiss of the regulator and the gentle drumming of exhaled bubbles. I hold a slender travel line between my fingertips; it connects ten screw eyes buried in the sand in the approximate shape of a ship's hull. The line is my connection to the world and I move along it, kicking gently with my fins.

My left hand sweeps across the rippled plain of silt as I continue. I take a pinch of the fine sand and roll it between my fingertips. I find no stones, no vegetation. The barrenness of the terrain, the blindness, and the soundless solitude is alien but in some way profoundly comforting. I close my eyes, abandoning everything to touch, and move more quickly, the line slithering easily between thumb and forefinger. Suddenly the searching hand encounters something sharp and solid in its path. My hand writhes reflexively at the enormity of the sensation and snaps back. I stare wide-eyed into the formless murk. I reach out again, following the bottom, until my knuckles come to rest against the toothy mass. I release the line and with both hands carefully proceed across its surface. Protruding from the silt, it is a piece of the seventeenth-century French wreck *La Belle*.

In January of 1686, the eighty-foot, three-masted *Belle*, a gift of Louis XIV to explorer René Robert Cavelier, Sieur de La Salle, was blown south by a storm across Matagorda Bay and sunk, some twelve miles northeast of present-day Port O'Connor. In what was hailed as "the most exciting nautical archaeology project ever in the U.S." by George Bass, the founder of underwater archaeology, Texas State marine archaeologist J. Barto Arnold III and his crew of professional archaeologists, students, and volunteers discovered the wreck in the summer of 1995. Arnold's search spanned some seventeen years.

Arnold, forty-six, began looking for the *Belle* in 1978, combing more than fifteen square miles of Matagorda Bay with a magnetometer over a period of two and a half months. The magnetometer was invented in World War II for use in antisubmarine warfare and mine detection, and measures variations—called "anomalies"—in the earth's magnetic field. Bodies of ferrous metal beneath the surface—submarines, or for the archaeologist, iron cannons or anchors— will betray themselves as spikes or mounds on a scrolling graph. While this initial search produced two other, less important wrecks, Arnold soon ran out of funding. Continuing research on the *Belle*, he did not return to the field until 1991. "We just had to find the wreck in the bay," he says. "All the documentation, all the archival information indicated it was there. The Spanish found it a year after it was wrecked. We just had to keep looking." With the help of donations, he expanded his search area in 1995 and discovered the site of the *Belle* within days.

Finding the wreck, says Arnold, was the most rewarding moment of his twenty-six-year career. In addition to the enormous significance of La Salle's expedition in Texan and

American history, he explains, very little is known about the design of the *Belle*'s class of ship—called a *barque longue*. As much as 20 percent of the hull may be preserved beneath the mud and sediment on the bay's bottom and will cast light on the techniques of seventeenth-century shipbuilding. Personal artifacts will reveal a wealth of unknown details about the lives of La Salle, the colonists, and crew. The rewards may be high, but finding such a site is hard work. "Underwater archaeology is eighty percent logistics," says Arnold. "Many people don't think of that. There's a lot of drudgery leading up to the fun. The thing that keeps you going are the 'Ah hah!' experiences. It's an incredible rush to shake the hand of someone from three hundred years ago."

Arnold, born and raised in San Antonio, considered a law career but decided on archaeology while an undergraduate at the University of Texas at Austin. He landed his first job in graduate school on the Padre Island project, conserving and later excavating the remains of a 1554 Spanish shipwreck off the coast of Texas. He sees his role as an archaeologist in great part as public service. "I get a real kick out of presenting all this to people," he says. "The *Belle* is a tremendously important site—not just personally but for everyone." Arnold recently joined a fifth-grade math lock-in, teaching students how math applies to archaeology through the measurement of lead shot taken from the *Belle*. Students wore white cotton gloves, divided the shot into two size groups, and averaged their diameters, a task standard to the trade. If Arnold shows a certain detachment from the objects of his search, it seems to lie in temperament and training. As he puts it, "The excitement is more intellectual than personal. From your first class in underwater archaeology, you are taught not to want to possess artifacts. If you skim off the surface, you're like a politician on the take." When not in the field, much of Arnold's work lies in politics, including fund-raising and professional service. A member of six professional archaeological organizations, he has served as president of the Society for Historical Archaeology and secretary-treasurer of the Society of Professional Archaeologists. He was also instrumental in the passage of the Abandoned Shipwreck Act of 1987, a federal law that gives states the right to protect shipwrecks older than fifty years from the predation of treasure hunters. Historic wrecks that lie outside national waters, however, enjoy no such protection, and may be salvaged by entrepreneurs with no training or respect for archaeology. Existing salvage law encourages individuals to return property of ships in peril to "the stream of commerce." The law, intended to apply to modern shipping, is manipulated by treasure hunters to protect their operations on historic sites. "It is an insane legal fiction," says Arnold, "to treat a two-hundred-year-old archaeological site like a ship that went down yesterday. Every underwater archaeologist spends a lot of time thinking, debating and fighting the treasure hunters, who are in it for themselves, for the money, and destroying our cultural heritage." Like bulldozing the

Roman Forum in search of precious metals, the historical losses of such operations are impossible to measure.

Now, in early May 1996, Arnold and his crew—a core of five plus a fluctuating number of volunteers—have returned to the wreck to explore and excavate a number of smaller sites detected in the vicinity of the *Belle*'s hull. Two boats lie at anchor on the site, some 500 yards north of the Matagorda peninsula—a narrow strip of sand, mesquite, and spartina marsh speckled with cattle and hunting cabins. The shallow bay is grey-green, opaque with sediment stirred up by weeks of unrelenting wind.

The *Michael Jean* is an abandoned shrimp fishing boat donated to the project for use as a diving platform. Her white hull is streaked with rust; bald tires hang from fraying lines along her sides. The floor and ceiling of the cramped wheel house are incompletely finished with three shades of bathroom linoleum tile. She is weary and neglected, but remains a pretty boat, well suited for the tasks at hand. A red and white diver down flag flies from the antenna. Eight or ten diving gear bags lie like fitted bricks in the center of the broad aft deck. A dozen electric blue scuba tanks lie in a neat row at the stern. Several five-gallon buckets, a cracked laundry basket, and a yellow ice chest, now empty, await artifacts. There is a scattering of lead diving weights, a perfectly coiled length of fire hose, a submersible metal detector, a gaspowered water pump, hand tools, gadgets, and assorted junk. Divers enter and exit the water in pairs.

From the deck of the *Michael Jean*, the May expedition will first address the so called Anomaly B, detected twenty-five yards southeast of the main wreck. Historical records indicate that a party of survivors attempted to escape with some of the ship's ordnance and stores on a raft. The raft never made it to shore; hope runs high that Anomaly B is its cargo. Anomaly C, yet farther to the east, may be one of the *Belle*'s anchors.

Beginning in late May; Arnold and his team will install a doubled-walled rectangular steel cofferdam around the hull remains, fill the space between the walls with sand, and drain the water from its center. The resulting structure, rising eight feet above the surface of the bay, will provide a substantial work platform and allow the crew to excavate the wreck in plain air. Only the third time a cofferdam has been employed in an archaeological context, a similar structure was used in the excavation of Henry VIII's warship *Mary Rose*.

In exploring the anomalies in early May, however, nothing is guaranteed. The divers may find armaments from the *Belle*'s raft, or they may find modern "artifacts," from contemporary fishing boats. At the very least, they must determine that the construction of the cofferdam will not endanger historical remains outside the perimeter of the main hull.

Over the next eight days, the crew attempts to pinpoint the anomalies. In a wetsuit and fins, assistant archaeologist

Layne Hedrick, twenty-eight, drags the magnetometer sensor, strapped to a Styrofoam surfboard, across the surface in the neighborhood of Anomaly B.

Hedrick, a graduate student at Texas A&M, recently spent three months on a team excavating the wreck of a seventeenth-century merchant vessel in the Red Sea, recovering hundreds of intact Chinese porcelain plates, African jugglets, and other trade items from Africa, India, and the Far East. Hedrick is president of the Southwest Underwater Archaeological Society (SUAS), an organization which trains certified divers as avocational underwater archaeologists. Similar organizations exist around the country for divers interested in acquiring first hand experience on historic sites. SUAS divers and other volunteers have provided ongoing support vital to the *Belle*'s excavation. Funds for the project remain sharply limited; Arnold's team depends largely on private monetary and in-kind donations.

Directing Hedrick's movements from the *Miss Kristi*, a transport vessel anchored near the *Michael Jean*, Arnold watches the needles rise and quiver on the scrolling graph. The highest reading taken on Anomaly B in 1995 was 150 gammas above normal. Hedrick kicks slowly over the site. "One forty," Arnold announces, his voice rising with excitement. "One fifty." The crew is quiet. "One sixty." The readings gradually decline until Arnold signals Hedrick to reverse directions. When the needle soars back to 160, Arnold shouts and Hedrick drops a weighted buoy on the position. Arnold leans back in his chair and smiles. "Far out," he says.

In the days that follow, divers work the site in pairs, sweeping the bottom with a metal detector, then dredging with a water-powered jet probe, its five-horsepower motor wailing on deck like a lawn mower. Crew members onboard watch the divers' air bubbles, log their dive times and air consumption, and take careful notes on all tasks as performed. Others fashion buoys from Gatorade bottles, organize artifact tags, and spray-paint clipboards to be used as underwater slates. Anomaly B continues to elude the divers, and a search for the anchor produces nothing but a wad of fishing net.

From the aft deck of the transport boat beside the *Michael Jean*, a quart of diet Coke in his hand, Arnold directs operations with the impenetrable detachment of a nineteenthcentury military commander. Larry Sanders, a senatorial aid and volunteer diver on the project, returns from a dive and hands Arnold a thin strip of seaweed for identification. "That," says Arnold, "is La Salle's shoelace."

To an archaeologist, I discover, there is no object—no matter how decrepit, or how commonplace—without potential use. There is nothing, apparently, that duct-tape cannot fix. Drawing from every trade and discipline from plumbing to computer science, the archaeologist, perpetually improvising, is the ultimate jerry-rigger. Every day poses new puzzles, new tasks for which no preexisting tool exists.

Underwater archaeology is still a new science, and they write the rule books as they proceed. This is one of the numerous appeals of the trade. "Nothing is ever standard in archaeology," says Arnold. "Nothing," appends archaeologist Laura Landry, "except the need to take meticulous notes." Landry, forty-one, made her first dig at sixteen, excavating the 1,200-year-old grave of an elderly woman from the Adena culture in Ohio.

The crew gathered for dinner ashore, Landry speaks with reverence of the profound connection she felt to the lost culture, and to the woman herself, during the excavation. The woman had been buried in fetal position, a bird bone necklace around her neck. The joints of her hands were swollen from arthritis. "I hope every archaeologist has such moments," says Landry, "that connect, that bridge this tremendous gap in time." Landry has volunteered on the project with her husband Jim Hauser, fifty-eight, a geologist, polybozologist, and the vice-president of the SUAS.

Bill Pierson, fifty-three, a seasoned diver, computer programmer, and the crew's Equipment and Logistics Manager, admits "a serious weakness for gadgets." Wearing a red T-shirt, shorts, and a Jack Daniel's bandanna secured like a pirate's kerchief on his head, Pierson says he retired last year to join the project. "I've died," he says, "and gone to heaven."

"It is often said in this business," says J. "Coz" Cozzi, assistant project director and doctoral candidate at Texas

A&M, "that you come up with a plan. And you abandon it almost immediately." Cozzi, thirty-nine, spent six years as a commercial diver before moving into underwater archaeology. Specializing in shipwrecks and hull reconstruction, he has worked extensively on the wrecks of sailing canal boats in Vermont's Lake Champlain. Commercial diving is a hazardous trade in which a moment's carelessness can kill; by temperament and training, Cozzi pays a more than rigorous attention to detail. The morning after he passed the night aboard the *Michael Jean*, standing guard over the site in his turn, the boat showed everywhere the evidence of recent industry: deck scrubbed, gear painstakingly reorganized, fraying ends of anchor lines tightly bound in coils of yellow twine.

Sara Keyes, twenty, a diver and archaeologist on the project, is a senior at the University of Texas and an assistant instructor at the Columbus Fleet Association's fifteenth-century sailing school in Corpus Christi. The school offers instruction in the navigation of scale reproductions of the *Niña, Pinta*, and *Santa Maria* and hopes to sail the fleet from Texas to New York Harbor. Keyes decided to become an underwater archaeologist at the age of six, after abandoning early career hopes in seventeenth-century piracy. She discovered the first pair of the Jesuit rings on the *Belle* and was with diver Chuck Meide when he found the cannon.

Aimée Green, twenty-six, abandoned a modeling career

in favor of an anthropology degree at the University of Texas. Now a senior and a diver/archaeologist on the *Belle* project, she shifted her focus to archaeology after spending a month in 1995 excavating Mayan ruins in the jungles of Belize. The crew cut single-file transit lines with machetes through dense jungle and discovered a large Mayan city. They uncovered a tomb beneath the floor of a temple chamber; Green and another student excavated bones and teeth from the hard clay with trowels and dental picks. After the ceaseless abstraction of academic anthropology, she was refreshed by the intense physical work and the contact with material remains.

The day before I joined the crew I studied a collection of artifacts collected from the site in 1995 with archaeologist and assistant project director Toni Carrell in a museum laboratory in Corpus Christi. In clear plastic organizing trays lay 236 bronze hawk bells—used to locate errant birds of prey in falconry—ranging in size from peas to marbles, many of them still paired by twisted strands of wire as fine as lightweight fishing line. Hand made in the Low Countries, the bells were brought as light, inexpensive trade goods for barter with the Indians. In other trays lay hundreds of brass wire pins, a pair of Jesuit rings, a boatswain's whistle, a bronze clasp, lead scatter shot, grind stones, scorched fire bricks from the *Belle*'s galley, a miraculously preserved wooden rigging block with a four-inch length of rope, a mysterious lead disk that Carrell believes was part of the ship's pump, and an object, still concealed beneath layers of shell and concreted mud and undergoing electrolysis, which resembles the head of a halberd.

The crowning discovery was the cannon. Five feet eleven inches long, 794 pounds of gleaming bronze, the gun was one of six four-pounders reported to have been aboard the *Belle*. After months of meticulous conservation, the barrel shows not a hint of age. The cannon is marked with the crests of Louis XIV and the Grand Admiral Le Comte de Vermandois, an illegitimate son of the king who assumed command of the French navy at age two. Forward of the breach are two lifting handles cast in a highly stylized, leonine interpretation of the "dolphins" by which such handles are known.

Spread out across a table lay twenty-three pewter plates, stamped with their maker's circular "touch mark" and identified as the property of one "L.G." Their owner is believed to be the Sieur Le Gros in La Salle's party. Le Gros was bitten by a rattlesnake while hunting snipe in the marshes surrounding Matagorda Bay and contracted gangrene; three months later, he died days after an inexperienced surgeon amputated the infected leg. The plates, confiscated by La Salle on Le Gros's death, were found in a neat stack within the hull's perimeter and lacked the scoring from cutlery commonly found in the surface of used pewter. This, Carrell explained, is good evidence that the plates had been manufactured for the anticipated French colony and were never used.

Two other pewter plates are marked instead with what appears to be a coat of arms. One of these is bent and heavily corroded. In the belly of the other can be seen the crosshatched markings of sustained use. With such a crest, the plates might well have been La Salle's. The oils from my skin will not harm the pewter and I lift it from the table. The tin and lead alloy is heavy, cool to the touch. I run a finger firmly down the longest of the cuts, mirroring the pressure of the blade that marked it.

La Salle was not, when all is said and done, a lucky man. Having discovered the mouth of the Mississippi and claiming half of the North American continent for France in 1682, he returned to the Gulf of Mexico two years later with some 300 soldiers and colonists aboard four ships with the intention of founding a permanent colony at the river's mouth. Losing one of the ships to Spanish pirates in the Caribbean, La Salle's fleet subsequently missed the great river by more than 400 miles—a blunder that continues to baffle historians—and arrived at Matagorda Bay in early 1685. Brilliant and driven, La Salle possessed an arrogance that made mortal enemies of his subordinates. Rather than obey La Salle's commands, one of his captains chose to run his ship, the *Aimable*, hopelessly aground while entering Matagorda Bay, sinking her in the Pass Cavallo and dealing the first death blow to the expedition. Matters did not improve from there. La Salle's third ship, *Le Joly*, returned to France for supplies and never returned. Founding Fort St.

Louis on the banks of the neighboring Garcitas Creek, La Salle continued northeast by canoe with fifty followers in search of the Mississippi. Guarded by a crew of eleven in La Salle's absence, the *Belle* awaited his return near the northeastern shore of Matagorda Bay. La Salle did not return on the date agreed, and five crewmen sent ashore for water vanished, almost certainly slain by natives. Out of water, the remaining crew resorted to the stores of wine and brandy. As days wore on with no sign of La Salle, the drunken, panicked crew of six decided to return to Fort St. Louis to the south. While under way, a storm blew the vessel south and drove her aground across the bay. Three of the crew struck for shore aboard a poorly fashioned raft and drowned. The remaining three crewmen, including a priest, built a second, superior raft, and made it safely ashore. Back at Fort St. Louis, colonists fell by the score to diseases, including syphilis, smallpox, and dysentery, until the fort was finally overrun and massacred by a local tribe. In 1687, at the age of forty-three, La Salle was assassinated by his own men between the Trinity and Brazos rivers. His body was stripped and left where it lay. A mere handful of survivors, including the expedition's chronicler, Joutel, returned to Canada on foot.

In eight days of diving from the *Michael Jean*, the expedition is successful in determining that no artifacts will be endangered by the cofferdam. But we are unable to locate either Anomaly B or the anchor. They may lie deeper in the silt than was expected, and the crew will continue the search with larger equipment later in the season. I, however, will see no piece of history stolen from the shallow depths of Matagorda Bay. At one point, a diver emerges with an object—the sole artifact found—rather like a chalice, choked with shells, concreted mud, and white coral. On closer inspection, dashing the excitement of the crew, the relic proves to be a twentieth-century flange. Such is the game.

THE TAMING
OF THE SAW

The problem, clearly, was the cold. The old lodge on the Beaverkill in which we planned to spend the winter was built in the 1920s, before the rising cost of oil created the need for three-paned glass and modern insulation. By today's standards, the once four-season lodge was now at best a summer home. There was a furnace of sorts, built for coal and later converted to burn oil at less than 40 percent efficiency. And the fireplace, a great stone maw that devoured all the fire's heat and a good deal more besides, was an even greater liability. When the wind blew across the chimney's mouth, it was like a giant pulling on a corncob pipe, and unless the flue was tightly shut, the pages of your book would flutter in the draw.

A wood stove seemed to be the answer.

We found a used one quickly enough, a friend's donation, its rusted interior still serving as the lodging for two mice and a decade's worth of shop debris. The mice crept gullibly into Havahart traps set with peanut butter (the rodents' bait of choice) and were bused to a lakeshore some miles to the east.

The wood was another matter. There was no shortage on the lot: Its forty-odd acres were thick with deadfall and standing maple, beech, and other hardwood, seasoned upright and ready to be felled, split, and stacked. But the bucksaw—a museum piece of my father's childhood, still hanging in the toolroom and sharp enough despite its years—could hardly keep up with the demand of the cold months ahead, which was estimated to be six or eight cords. When our friend the stove donor threw in the offer of a chain saw for the season, I readily accepted.

A chain-saw operator can fell and section a tree for splitting in a fraction of the time required with axe and manual saw. Hard work, of course, was part of the appeal of the place, but we had no hydraulic splitter. All work with wedge and maul would still be done by hand. By my reckoning, splitting six or eight cords over the coming months would constitute an adequate amount of outdoor labor.

And yet the chain saw holds a particular position in the average suburban-bred psyche. It wasn't an aspect of daily life in the town of my childhood, where firewood arrived in the back of a dump truck, paused briefly on the back porch, and made its way into the fire.

Instead the tool was a film prop. Who can erase the image of the manchild in *The Texas Chainsaw Massacre*? The tool performs a grisly task in *Scarface*—"Naow zee leg, hunh?"—and is given a walk-on part in many other movies. Hollywood has branded the chain saw an embodiment of psychosis and unbridled mayhem. And the machine provides its own sound effects—a roar almost as terrifying and aggressive as images of the blade in contact with flesh.

The chain saw's portrayals in legend do little to allay one's sense of its inherent malevolence. The tale of the logger pinned beneath a fallen tree of impossible diameter, forced to cut one or both legs off with the tool and then drag himself, like Monty Python's Black Knight, legless through thirty miles of icy woods, is subject to infinite and often epic variation.

A new bar and chain were required for the beat-up saw, so I took it to the saw dealer, a neighbor who works out of his home. On his mantelpiece stood a row of gleaming figures, each holding high a golden laurel wreath. I read the engraved plaques on marble bases: FIRST PLACE, COUNTY

CHAINSAW COMPETITION, 1987. SECOND PLACE, THIRD PLACE, FIRST PLACE, 1988, 1989, 1990. Chain-saw trophies from one end of his mantelpiece to the other.

"All won with this saw right here. The one I work with." He indicated a large German model sitting smugly in its open case.

He produced a stack of calendars, each month a different saw, a different champion. He opened one to reveal the present world champ in the custom class. The man held a modified saw the size of a truck engine, huge exhaust pipes sweeping back, the bar three-quarters through a horizontal log. Smoke and sawdust filled the atmosphere behind the champion. Sweat ran down his arms.

"Twenty-inch-diameter pine," the dealer said.

"How long did he take to make the cut?"

"Two seconds. At the outside."

He looked down at the pictured saw with unconcealed awe and shook his head.

"Nothing like it. I tell you, you should go to one of these saw competitions. It'll change your life."

With the new bar and chain came a thin booklet on chain-saw handling, a welcome document that I read carefully twice before setting hand to saw. It warned of the physics of the beast—the infamous kickback, caused by several possible circumstances but most notably the tip's catching on another surface. This can send the machine careering up and into a face or throat, its power diverted from the chain into the body of the saw. Other possibilities, less vivid but still formidable, were laid out simply, the precautions to be taken clear. To clarify the potential of kickback, the saw dealer had zealously dealt me another anecdote, this one with the legitimacy of a professional source.

An acquaintance of his stopped one evening to cut up a tree lying dead by the side of the road. He worked quickly in the dimming light, eager to get home, and didn't see the burl waiting for his blade. With a quick jerk, the saw kicked back and fell to the ground from his hands. "That was close," he said to himself and reached down to continue the job. Then he felt the warmth from the severed carotid artery in his torn throat, and he lay down on the roadside to die. The next moment he reconsidered—there were children, a young wife—and with a balled-up rag pressed against the wound, he tried to make it into town. He chanced to come up behind an off-duty ambulance and was saved. By the time they got him stitched up, he had lost more than half his blood.

I finished the safety booklet and set out with heavy tread for the woodpile. Wearing shatterproof glasses, stout orange silencers, and rawhide gloves, I felt underprepared for an event that seemed to warrant a great heaume, hauberk, and greaves. I started the saw with a tug, ready for a kickback to beeline for my vitals. Spared evisceration in the starting, I poised for the first cut while the engine warmed. Several moments passed. Perhaps I should move the woodpile into the garage first, I mused, what with the coming of rain ... Coward! Make the damn cut! The teeth nibbled delicately on the bark. Small chips flecked against my boots. The manual had advised that I operate at maximum rpm to reduce the possibility of kickback. With the trigger clenched and the engine howling at full throttle, the teeth took another taste. Bare wood gleamed; the dust blew golden on my pant cuffs. I allowed the saw to take long, steady gulps of the seasoned beech, snarling, vibrating deep into my upper arm, deceptively still, descending slowly and easily through the narrow width.

The section tumbled off into the leaves and the saw took a breath. I released the trigger. *Hum-a-ding-ding-ding-a-ding-ding*—it idled pleasantly like any healthy two-stroke motorcycle engine. I examined the chain, now still and wet with oil. The dust that had gathered where the chain slinks into the machine's innards was wet and gummy, like sedimenting grass on the bottom of a lawn mower.

Soon the pile was cut to length, the weapon more comfortable, if still unwelcome, in the hand. With the light step of a man who has cheated death, I stacked the hour's quick work and made it back inside as the first raindrops fell. The stove was fed for the night.

In the weeks to come, I would tame the saw, learn its nature, acknowledge the enormous boost in productivity. I raced the stove and soon outstripped it. The woodpiles climbed faster than they could be devoured. Trees fell by the dozens, suddenly. Deadfall simply disappeared.

And now the fear of the machine is gone, leaving only the respect required for safe use. The chain saw is no longer a film prop but a simple tool that has saved hours of hard work.

And how I hate the thing: its roar, its stink, its jarring vibration, its very presence a transgression in the quiet of the woods. Perhaps most of all I dislike its efficiency. I now understand the mulish refusal of Tolstoy's serfs to give up their antiquated tools. It's more than a question of aesthetics, of an offended ear or nose. Nor is it simply stubbornness—that what is new must be worse. I suppose it's the intuitive awareness that what relieves us of our labor removes us from our lives. We grow more frail and dim-witted with each invention that outstrips us. It is this sense of robbery, of loss, that makes us cringe at technology's advance.

And yet the bucksaw hangs in the garage. We simply need the wood.

WINTER PASSAGE

Before dawn at the Portsmouth Marine Terminal in Norfolk, Virginia, huge cranes stand motionless on the pier. A city of steel containers stretches across the terminal's concrete plain. Twenty or forty feet in length, the containers are stacked in long rows four or five stories high. A cold wind rolls across the harbor from the north. Across the water lie American warships. There are carriers, destroyers, cruisers, submarines, battleships in fine, glittering arcs of yellow and white lights.

At six-forty, the lights of the container ship *California Senator* appear out of the darkness to the north. She is moving fast, a tugboat nudging her at either side. A third tug follows in her wake. Her decks are neatly jammed with containers four and five high. Bremen-built, German-owned, the container ship is 708 feet long and weighs—fully loaded—some 48,000 tons.

The tugs turn the ship in a circle and push her port side against the dock. Dockworkers receive lines thrown by the ship's crew. The *Senator* is tied off by seven thirty-six. Three orange cranes slide on tracks into position. By 8 A.M., it has started to drizzle, and the containers are coming off three at a time.

I climb the gangway and five flights of stairs to my cabin. Once an officer's stateroom, the cabin is dark but roomy at nineteen square meters, with a private shower and toilet. There is a couch and coffee table, a desk, an empty fridge, its freezer choked with frost. Two windows face the bow.

I have booked this cabin to Valencia, Spain. For an average of $100 a day, freighters are comfortable but not luxurious. Some merchant vessels have small indoor pools, weight rooms, and communal VCRs.

I lean in my window and watch the cranes. They are pulling containers off the ship like three dogs digging holes in the sand.

Giant "straddle carriers" swarm about the cranes' legs. Shaped like inverted U's, they fetch and deliver containers to the cranes. In the steel canyons of container ports, straddle carriers appear suddenly and at great speeds around corners. Orange, wheeled variations of Imperial walkers in the *Star Wars* universe, they represent the greatest danger on a working pier. Cars and small trucks are typically crushed flat in collisions. More longshoremen are killed by straddle carriers in American ports than any other single hazard. For this reason, the machines are equipped with flashing lights and alarms that sound incessantly: a shrill, plaintive twitter that is somehow pleasing to the ear. On the *Senator*'s last voyage, the ship's boatswain took his last step off the ship's gangway in the port of Busan, Korea, and into the fatal path of a straddle carrier.

The containers are green or blue, rust or umber, tan or grey. They are marked on their sides in white letters with names like Hanjin, Cho Yang, Florens, Tiphook. With a volume of 2,390 cubic feet, a fully loaded forty-foot container weighs more than 33 tons.

The cranes are pulling off containers said to contain ladies' wear, electrical goods, office chairs, Egyptian fennel, sofas, axles, drain pumps, sandals, artichoke hearts, yarn, and French mineral water. There is also a container bearing 7,936 pounds of the personal effects of a Mr. and Mrs. Feissel of Nicosia, California.

Lunch aboard ship is at eleven-thirty—prepared by the ship's cook, Toby Gargallo. The cuisine, by and large, reflects less Gargallo's Filipino culinary heritage than the ship's

German flag. In this respect, things could certainly be worse; it could be a British ship. Served with what is usually a meat of unknown provenance in a brown sauce, there are bread and cheese, a plain salad, steamed potatoes, anemic beans. My fellow passengers seem satisfied, and one of them, a German veteran of more than fifteen freighter journeys, later claims that this is the best food he's ever had aboard a working ship. Once or twice, Gargallo produces filets of red snapper in a sweet, peppery sauce of the Philippines. There is roast chicken one evening, pan pizza another. The lone cook in his small galley is neither expected nor prepared to dazzle passengers or crew. But within the repetitive limits of the established menu, Gargallo clearly makes an effort. Before going to sea to better support his wife and three children, he worked as a chef at a luxury hotel in Manila.

At dinner, I meet fellow passenger Peta Collivet from Greenwich Village. Collivet boarded yesterday in New York and will disembark at the same port after a round trip voyage of eighty-nine days. Before this trip, Collivet went around the world on an open cargo ship. In 1948, then an English eighteen-year-old art school graduate, Collivet joined what would later become the World Health Organization. She made three trips as an escort officer on converted troop ships, bearing concentration camp refugees from ports in Europe to the prospect if not the promise of new lives in Australia and New Zealand. Departing from Amsterdam and Naples and Bremen, each ship took hundreds of Jewish refugees and supporting personnel.

Many of the refugees would resettle successfully and start families. Others were less fortunate. "There is one young woman I will never forget," Collivet tells me over dinner. "She was very young, perhaps eighteen, and very pretty. I believe she was French. She had no surviving family, and she had gone mad in the camp. She had clearly been terribly mistreated. In the tropics, the refugees would gather on the deck to stay cool, and she would dance. There was no music—but she would dance, and as she danced she would take her clothes off. We tried to calm her down—but nothing seemed to help. One day, in the Indian Ocean, she danced slowly to the edge of the deck, removing her clothes, and jumped off. They stopped the ship immediately and began to turn around, but before they could get a boat into the water, she was gone.

"Sharks followed the ship in the tropics, because every day the crew threw garbage overboard. It was very fast. Everybody rushed to the rail and watched helplessly, and by the time I got there she was gone. All I could see were the fins. She didn't even cry out."

At midnight, wind beats the windows of my cabin with rain. Outside, beneath the yellow lights, the giant machines are still working. The straddle carriers chirp and the cranes groan and like a distant, irregular drum, *boom . . . boom . . . boom*, the containers keep coming on.

———

The ship's engines rumble awake at six o'clock, before dawn, and by the time I make it to the bridge we are passing the American warships across the harbor. Whiting Chisolm stands in the middle of the bridge, watching the water, and calls out a series of short commands. The helmsman, standing at a wheel not ten inches in diameter, echoes these orders as he obeys them.

"Half ahead," says Chisolm.

"Half ahead, sir," says the helmsman, adjusting the throttle.

"Starboard ten," says Chisolm.

"Starboard ten, sir," says the helmsman, adjusting the helm.

"Very well," says Chisolm.

Chisolm is one of thirty-eight pilots certified to operate in Virginia waters. Following a college education and five years of apprenticeship, he received his pilot's license from the U.S. Coast Guard and the State of Virginia. I ask him if he sees the bottom of the harbor before us as if it were drained of water.

"I see numbers," he says.

In the course of his training, as required, he redrew all the charts of Norfolk Harbor, twice. There is no dress code for ship's pilots or nonmilitary seamen. Rolf-Dietrich Krach, the fifty-two-year-old captain of the *California Senator*, wears jeans and a sweatshirt. He and his German chief officer, thirty-six-year-old Jens-Uwe Möschter, sit at the helm, forward of the standing helmsman. At the captain's request, the ship's steward brings breakfast to the pilot.

At eight-forty, past Cape Henry, Chisolm disembarks. He descends a short rope ladder onto a waiting pilot boat, waves at the *Senator*'s bridge, and ducks into the boat's small cabin.

The ship rounds Cape Hatteras and heads south, into the Gulf Stream, toward Savannah. Country music plays on the bridge radio. At eight o'clock, Chief Officer Möschter was replaced by Third Officer Narciso Hinahon. A native of the Philippines, the forty-two-year-old Hinahon spends an average of nine months a year at sea. He has missed the births of each of his four children.

At 3 P.M., I find Chief Engineer Uwe Dedek and Ship's Mechanic Jorg Appeldorn smoking over coffee at a small, fixed table beneath a round porthole in the ship's central office, one deck above the engine room.

The smoke curls in the bright afternoon light that comes through the porthole. A native of the former East Germany, the thirty-year-old Dedek has been aboard the *Senator* for six and a half months. On January 24, he will disembark in La Spezia, Italy, for a three-month vacation. He is counting the days. He is also counting the hours. "Fourteen and hours," he says. He is unmarried and has a twelve-year-old daughter whom he rarely sees. Six feet tall and broad-shouldered, dressed in an engineer's red pullover, he has a handshake that could powder pool balls.

Appeldorn could powder Dedek. He is six foot three and weighs 230 pounds, but these figures do little to suggest his mass. Descended from Swedish settlers on Germany's Baltic coast, Appeldorn is blond, blue-eyed, and mustached, and at thirty-eight resembles a Viking approaching an early retirement. A truck driver's son, he started work at fifteen, as a carpenter's apprentice, and went to sea at twenty. For two years he worked on small fishing boats in the Baltic and North Sea, then signed up on a freighter as an able-bodied seaman. He has been a ship's mechanic since 1987. He wears blue overalls, two gold hoops in one ear, and a gold chain around his neck. His hands and forearms are scarred, and covered with tattoos. There is a Pegasus, a butterfly, the portrait of a blonde, a square-rigger between the wings of an eagle, a shamrock, a Chinese dragon, a small heart, a star. Across the knuckles of one hand is the four-letter name of an ex-girlfriend. The finest and most recent tattoo is a rendering of Yosemite Sam. Three inches high from hat to heel, the cartoon character is blowing the foam from a mug of beer.

Among shipmates, his nickname is "Rehlein," or "Doe." Unmarried, he lives with his parents when ashore. Last July, surgeons removed an apparently benign tumor the size of an egg from behind Appeldorn's left eye. The headaches have returned, however, and are worsening, and Appeldorn suspects that he will undergo a second surgery in March. Aboard the *Senator*, he often works an eighteen-hour day. He has been at sea for three and a half months.

The *California Senator* is owned by Niederelbe Schiffahrtsgesellschaft Buxtehude, mercifully reduced to NSB. Based in Buxtehude, Germany, NSB is the fourth-largest container shipping company in the world, and owns nearly sixty ships. German wage and insurance laws make all-German crews financially difficult to justify, and all of their vessels have split German and Filipino crews. While the ship appears to run well—in thirteen days aboard, I never witness a single exchange of hostility—there is some cultural friction between the two groups. The ship's German crew includes the captain, the first and second officers, the chief and second engineers, two ship's mechanics, and a mechanic's apprentice. Among the Filipinos are the third officer, third engineer, boatswain, four able-bodied seamen, three "oilers," who work in the engine room, the ship's lone steward, and the cook. There is no radio operator, no purser, no ship's doctor, no carpenter, and no storekeeper—all positions commonly filled on merchant ships in generations past. In 1965, a large cargo vessel might have had a crew of thirty or more, including several stewards. With increased computerization and a broader range of responsibilities among the officers, the *Senator* gets by on twenty, and the open cabins are offered to paying passengers.

Working for a large company has its advantages; on a fleet

of sixty ships, there is almost always work. Indeed, the fleet has more positions than reliable crewmen and officers to fill them. A bigger fleet also has its drawbacks. Foremost among them, to hear the sailors tell, is the fact that the crews are always changing. Dedek has worked for NSB for eight years; in that time, he has returned to a familiar vessel only once, and when he did the crew had changed entirely. With crews in constant flux, trust is slower to develop. The sailors don't expect to see each other again. On a smaller fishing boat, a sailor can work for fifteen or twenty years with much the same crew. But on a fleet of sixty, says Appeldorn, you can spend eight or ten years before you run into a sailor you know.

I thank them for the coffee and step out on deck, into the wind. Here, in the center of the Gulf Stream, the water temperature is nearly seventy-five degrees Fahrenheit—more than thirty degrees warmer than the forty-degree air. As far as the eye can see, the rolling ocean steams like a hot spring. A dense, ragged mist, called sea smoke, pools in the bowls between black swells, swirls and tugs along their foam-capped crests. The ocean appears bewitched, as if surrendering the shades of the drowned.

I move forward along the companionway and climb a ladder into the cargo. Narrow passages cut through the stacks of containers, and in their midst I find an open, sunlit clearing, walled on all sides by the containers. Like a small sandstone canyon, the artificial glade provides a sense of privacy. Were it not for the oil and grime and salt spotting the grey steel deck, it would be a fine place—four high walls beneath a cloud-swept sky—to lie down and take a nap.

As the ship moves through the gentle, three-foot swells, her steel frame flexes imperceptibly along its axis, like a washcloth being wrung between two hands. This causes the ship's rigid steel hatch covers, concealed by the containers, to shift with explosive, staccato reports in their frames, like an AK-47 firing blanks inside a church bell.

On the bridge the following morning, Captain Krach inspects his charts, spins the silver steel legs of the dividers along the pencil line that crosses the Atlantic in a broad arc, and makes a prediction; "Savannah to Valencia—nine days, nine hours—pier to pier." Having been battered by six days of storms on their last crossing, the ship arrived in New York—and then Norfolk—two days behind schedule. This is all too common, and passengers must plan accordingly. Ships leave "on or around" their scheduled dates. Occasionally, severe storms or mechanical problems will delay ships for weeks.

The captain's prediction is based on an average sea speed across the Atlantic of nineteen knots. "A bit optimistic," he concedes. "But we must always be optimistic." Conditions permitting, the *Senator*'s maximum speed is twenty-one knots. Wind, current, and swell can all slow a ship down. Going in the right direction, they can also push it along.

Oceanic wind patterns move in spirals. While navigating a course, adjustments are made daily, even hourly, to keep the wind astern.

Late in the morning, we enter the Savannah River, gliding through a broad channel defined by rock jetties. A low, brick fort stands at the river's mouth. Its walls still pocked by cannon fire, Fort Pulaski was built by the Confederates to defend the river early in the Civil War. In 1862, Union warships, equipped for the first time with rifled cannons from France, anchored just out of range of the Confederate smoothbore artillery and pounded the fort with impunity until the Confederates surrendered. When William Tecumseh Sherman arrived overland two years later, in his infamous, incendiary March to the Sea, the fate of Savannah was sealed.

The mouth of the river is surrounded by protected marshland, thick with scrub brush, pine, cedar, and oak. Alligators reputedly occupy the river in great numbers. I stand on the wing and scan the opaque surface of the water along the banks for suspicious logs. If there are alligators out in early January, I don't see them. As the ship motors easily along the narrow river, its wake works the shorelines with insidious power. The ship creates a hole in the river and drains the water from the banks as it approaches. The water recedes like a swift tide, widening the beaches and exposing sandy shallows to the air. In the warmer months, the river's beaches are populated by bathers and fishermen. Children, excited by the sudden tide, often run out across the flats to look for shells. Fishermen, seated in rowboats, find themselves suddenly aground. They look up in time to see the three- to six-foot wall of water, the leading rail of the ship's wake, rolling across the flats and the dry beach with enough speed and force to flip their small crafts and sweep them all—fishermen, children, sunbathing parents—into the river. In this way, despite reduced shipping speeds, public advisories, horn blasts, and shouting crewmen, children and adults are killed or injured every year by freighter traffic on the Savannah River. In winter, the beaches are abandoned. The curved, rolling walls of water, moving apace with the *Senator*, do nothing but a little housekeeping.

We soon pass under the bridge in downtown Savannah, turn full circle with the help of two tugboats, and dock at the enormous container port with our bow downriver. It is a clear, warm day, and while the cranes set to work, I disembark with Peta Collivet and the ship's cook and catch a taxi into town for supplies. Tony Carrierre, our driver, often takes seamen into downtown Savannah. When he drives them back, at four or five in the morning, they are often unable to remember the names of their ships. Before they nod off, Carrierre asks for their shore passes. The Port Authority provides the names and locations of their vessels. Sometimes Carrierre helps carry the unconscious crewmen aboard.

We pass through a checkpoint as we leave the port. An agent in a booth glances at our passports, asks a few questions, and waves us on. This is primarily to prevent foreign sailors from jumping ship, Carrierre explains. A perennial problem in nearly any American port, it was rife in Savannah in the mid-1980s.

A friend of Carrierre's drove four Venezuelan sailors from the foot of a ship's gangway in Savannah to a California street corner for $800 apiece. Offhand, this sounds like a lot of money—$3,200 for a taxi ride—but I wonder why the driver took the chance. Aiding illegal immigrants is a felony, for one, and if you knock nearly $1,800 off the fee for fuel and wear to the car (at 29 cents a mile), the driver only netted $1,400 for a minimum of eight or ten days' work. It's hard to believe that the same driver working downtown Savannah couldn't clear more than $200 on a decent shift. Maybe I overestimate. Maybe the driver just liked the idea of coming home and laying more than $3,000 on his kitchen table. Maybe he wanted to help the sailors out. In any case, they paid cash in advance, and after a quick stop at the driver's home to drop off the fare—the third condition of the agreement—they drove to downtown Los Angeles.

I ask Carrierre why ship jumpers don't just take a cab to a bus station and buy a seat across country for $100. "That's the first place the authorities look," he says. "Airports, train stations, bus stations. They always catch them if they try it locally. Some of them get cabs to Atlanta and take their chances from there."

In town, we gather supplies—mangoes, avocados, and other items unlikely to materialize in the ship's store or galley between here and Valencia.

After dinner, I find four of the German crewmen in the officers' lounge. We are scheduled to depart not long after midnight, and the crew has no time, realistically, for a trip into town. Not all freighters, of course, carry containers; there are "ro-ro's" (for "roll-on roll-off") that carry nothing but cars, and open cargo ships, that carry anything from huge machines to grain in their holds and on their decks. Given the irregularity of open cargo, such ships take longer to load and unload than container ships, and typically spend at least a few days in every port. While less efficient than containers and perhaps less profitable, this gives the crews and passengers of open cargo ships a fighting chance of spending an evening or two ashore. On most container ships, the *Senator* included, they are in and out of port so fast—usually in less than a day—that most of the crewmen don't get off work in time for a run into town. Weeks can pass before crewmen step off the boat.

The air in the lounge is nearly opaque with cigarette smoke. Green bottles of Beck's beer stand on the bar. Appeldorn is there, with fellow mechanic Jan Boden, Second Engineer Kurt Glaser, and Appeldorn's apprentice, Rene

Laschewski. I pull up a stool at the end of the bar. Boden, seated on a stool behind the bar, reaches into a small fridge beneath the bar, withdraws a bottle of Beck's, uncaps it, and places it before me on the bar. On a sheet of paper, beside his name, in a column marked "Bier," he makes a single mark beside a score of similar marks—every four lines barred by a fifth—like scratches on a cell wall. There are other columns, predominantly empty, for Coke and tonic. They drink their beers in silence, throwing the empties with near shattering force into the plastic garbage can in one corner behind the bar. To a man, they look like they'd rather be somewhere else.

Directly across the hall is the crews' lounge, similarly equipped but smaller and more primitive than the officers'. Officially designated in terms of rank, the two lounges divide in practice along cultural lines. Thus the apprentice Laschewski, with a fraction of the responsibility of Third Officer Hinahon, drinks at the same bar, by preference, as the chief mate. Hinahon, by preference, drinks in the crews' lounge with his countrymen. This natural pattern typically repeats itself on other ships. "For this crew," the captain later tells me, "this is all right. But I have had officers come to me and say, 'I am an officer, and I will not have the ship's mechanic in the officers' bar.' So I must say to the mechanic, I am sorry, but you must go to the other bar.' "

Appeldorn retires early, and then Boden. After midnight I leave Glaser and Laschewski in the bar and mount to the bridge. The cranes are slowing down; we will sail well before dawn. At twelve-thirty the captain appears.

"Good morning," he says brightly. He pauses in front of a wall calendar and slides a red plastic square, the date's indicator, from the eleventh to the twelfth of January. He taps the twenty-third of the month with a fingertip. Bright red arrows arc across the calendar from all four corners to point at this date. If this were not enough to indicate its importance, the twenty-third has been circled, three times, with broad highlighter pens: pink within blue within yellow. On the twenty-third, like Dedek, Krach will disembark in La Spezia. After six months at sea, he will fly home to his wife in Germany for three months of vacation.

I join him at the helm. We watch the cranes. He smokes a pipe, tamps it with a rectangular ivory plug from China. Carved into one side of the plug, an exotic bird rests in the boughs of a flowering cherry tree.

I ask him if he has ever been forced to abandon a ship at sea.

"No," he says. "Everything else. Storms, fires, collisions, pirates. But I have never had to leave a ship."

By five the following morning, we have left Savannah and move back downriver through the darkness, past the marshes, under the direction of pilot Mike Foran. The air temperature is forty degrees; a light wind blows across the marsh. Through a clear sky, the light of a fine crescent moon reflects dimly from the tops of the containers. Fixed to a tower on the foredeck, a single, blue steering light is visible at the ship's bow. Seen from the bridge, the light is the size of Venus, and about as bright. A twenty-foot band of sharply delineated foam, dense as the golden cream on the top of an espresso, runs along the ship's hull from bow to stern and beyond, where it forms the swirling margin of the engine's wake. Outside the band of foam the surface of the river is smooth, impenetrable, a green so dark it's nearly colorless. Beyond the foam, gently curving swells sweep out away from the hull like folds of skin. From the ship's bridge, moving at the same speed, the swells appear motionless. It is only at their tips, where they break along the shore, that their movement is perceived.

Foran joins me, and I ask him what he likes most about piloting. "Last night," he answers, "I kissed my kids goodnight and lay down around seven. I got up at midnight. I'll be back in time to send them to school.

"It's the best job in the industry," he says. "You get to go home."

The *Senator* moves down the river like a locomotive on a cushion of air. There is only the deep vibration of the engine, now amplified in reflection off the river bottom.

At five thirty-five, we pass Fort Pulaski to starboard. At the same moment, another container ship, heading upriver, passes us to port. We have emerged from the river and now follow the channel, between the jetties.

At six o'clock, the faintest, finest thread of orange appears along the eastern horizon. A band of pale grey gradually expands above it, grading into the night sky. We leave the jetties behind and pass the first channel markers. The markers blink green and red. Their bells clang dimly in the ship's wake. Astern, Savannah is no more than a belt of yellow lights.

While I grew up in boats and crossed the Atlantic on the S.S. *France* at the involuntary age of six months, I have never made a conscious oceanic crossing by sea. For whatever reasons, I usually feel more comfortable on or in the water than on land. And I know that this ship, and others like it, have crossed the Atlantic over and over again. And yet, as I look back at the Georgia coast, at the narrow string of warm lights, beyond the marsh, and then look back at the empty horizon of the open sea—with the knowledge that we are heading out, *across*, and not following, however distantly, a coastline—I feel a visceral objection to the thought, a powerful desire to turn back. As long as we sail, my intuition tells me, we will never reach another shore. Should we sink, we will glide interminably through a bottomless darkness.

I remind myself that I'm standing on the bridge of a 700-foot-long steel container ship, eleven months shy of 2000. I try to imagine how the crew of the *Santa Maria* felt about the same Atlantic in 1492. No Loran, no radio, no charts. No technology, by our standards; only faith. They were just a handful of men who couldn't swim, setting out across an uncharted ocean in a wooden ship that had less chance in a squall than the *Senator*'s lifeboat, just waiting to fall off the edge of the flat world.

At twenty after six, Foran prepares to disembark. He comes out to the wing, shakes my hand. "God bless you," he says in parting. I have heard these words before, of course, and he may have said them reflexively. In context they strike me like a brand.

When the pilot has disembarked, I go back into the bridge, out of the cold. We steam eastward.

"So we have passed the last marker," I say to the captain.

"Yes," he replies. "That was the sea buoy. After that, nothing."

A winter crossing of the so-called Great Circle route in the middle North Atlantic is the most notorious and unpredictable passage in world shipping. North Atlantic storms can and occasionally do sink freighters, and when that happens, the crew is often doomed. One acquaintance in the United States merchant marine said he has never seen so many hardened men so pitifully afraid as the crew of a freighter in a big Atlantic storm. Waves as high as the fifth-story bridge pounded the ship and swept thirty-ton containers into the sea like children's blocks. With the hull rolling forty-five degrees in both directions, the crew worked furiously to keep the massive engines running. A breakdown in the engine room or a failed rudder—anything that might eliminate the ship's ability to maintain steerage and keep her bow into the seas—would have finished them. A ship without steerage in a storm of that caliber would be broadsided, rolled, and sunk. They had no choice but to ride it out—the lifeboats had gone over with the containers.

Most of the crewmen aboard the *Senator* have been in storms where they feared for their lives—often for days at a time. More than once, Captain Krach has seen veteran officers standing on the bridge in a huge storm with tears streaming down their faces. At the tail end of 1992, Appeldorn was aboard an NSB container ship heading north from Miami to New York. A storm hit them off Cape Hatteras—hurricane force winds, swells in excess of forty or fifty feet—and for six days they struggled simply to stay afloat. Appeldorn didn't sleep for four days. "It took three of us to make coffee," he says. "One to hold the pot, another to hold the filter, and a third to pour—*very* carefully."

The captain leaves the bridge before sunrise, and I spend the early morning on the bridge with Möschter. Möschter started his career at sixteen in the East German navy, but left the navy for shipping because he likes being at sea. "In Germany, if you want seafaring," he says, "you must leave the navy. You must be in shipping. In Germany, the navy stays at port." Möschter married at nineteen; the marriage failed, he says, because his wife could not withstand his long absences. After the divorce, he suspected that she entertained not one but two lovers while he was at sea. He has two teenage sons by that marriage but hasn't seen or heard from them in years. "I write to them," he says, "but I guess they do not want to write back."

Under sail, a thirty-foot sloop passes the *Senator* close to port.

"Small vessels like that are the greatest danger," Möschter observes. "They do not appear on radar and have small lights."

Off the coast of Brazil, at night or in the fog, he has passed small fishing boats sixty or eighty miles from shore, with nothing but a single, yellow gas lamp swinging in their bows.

I finally retreat to my cabin, blasted with fatigue, and sleep fitfully through midafternoon. There is no roll or pitch of the ship in the flat seas, and I have all but lost awareness of the incessant vibration.

Shortly after four o'clock, I find Dedek, Glaser, Appeldorn, and Laschewski amid the containers, perched on a wooden scaffold and two ladders and working on a broken compressor. The compressor runs the cooling unit for a "reefer," or refrigerating container, and the reefer's contents—20 tons of apples, loaded in New York, bound for La Spezia—must be kept at freezing or they will spoil. Although the ship is not officially liable, and the apples are insured, the *Senator*'s crew must do their best to maintain the reefer.

Time appears to be running out; apple juice snakes along the deck beneath the container, into drifts of sawdust scattered by Laschewski.

I mount to the bridge shortly before sunset. It is summer weather, and the captain is dressed in thin khaki pants and shirtsleeves. As he is often to be found, he is leaning on the rail on the starboard wing, watching the sea. He turns and greets me, gestures to the sinking sun.

"Have you ever seen the green flash?"

I tell him I haven't.

"Very rarely, when the sun sets, at the last moment that it sinks beneath the horizon"—he draws his fingers to a point and opens them like a blossom. "*Ffffut*. A bright green flash. And then it's gone. It may happen only once or twice in a long voyage. Some sailors have never seen it." He regards the orange sun. "Maybe tonight."

Half an hour later, when the sun drops beneath the horizon, the captain is watching from the wing. But there is no green flash.

At five o'clock, the passengers meet with Second Officer Thomas for a safety meeting in the ship's central office. We put on our lifejackets, rectangular orange blocks with reflecting panels, whistles, and small lights. He tells us to hold the jackets down if we jump into the sea and bring up our knees, to keep the jacket from breaking our necks on impact with the water. "If you do not do this, you will be floating," he says cheerfully, "but you will be dead." He shows us our mustering station on the third deck, the other, self-opening lifeboats in white containers, life rings, and the "free-fall lifeboat" which can hold thirty and is used for standard evacuation of the ship. The free-fall boat can be launched and driven by the second officer from within. Inside, the seats are padded, with foam blocks surrounding the head and cross-body harnesses. The boats are designed to take any conceivable beating at sea. The second officer and others tested it recently, in port, and report that it was like an amusement park ride. When I first saw it, and peered within, it struck me as the perfect place to stowaway. Indeed, they recently discovered two stowaways inside it.

On the landing at the bottom of the stairs on the mess deck hangs a wooden sign: TONIGHT CLOCKS MOVE FORWARD ONE HOUR. This sign will hang there nearly every evening until we land in Spain. Hour by hour, day after day, we are shiplagged. Möschter is convinced that the endless nickel and diming of the ship's clock is harder to adjust to than the swifter changes of air travel. The effect is certainly more insidious than I had imagined. No problem, I thought, until breakfast at seven-thirty started feeling like two in the morning.

After dinner, I join the Philippine crew in the crew's lounge. Six of them are playing tong-its, a Philippine card game, while others look on. American coins are laid on the table in small piles. Third Officer Hinahon plays at one table. Most of the crewmen wear rubber sandals and shorts.

Beneath a four-foot decorated plastic Christmas tree, standing on a side counter, two full bottles of Beck's jingle together from the ship's vibration. A minority of the crewmen are drinking beer from open bottles. A few of them smoke.

Soon after, the captain invites me to his cabin for a beer. Krach has been sailing since the age of twenty-one. He calls his wife of twenty-four years from every port, and they speak once or twice a week via the ship's satellite phone.

At seven-forty, the phone rings. The compressor for the reefer is running; the apples are saved.

The most difficult aspect of Krach's job, he says, is handling the crew.

"Sometimes one member of the crew works very hard, and another does not, and the first comes to me and says so-and-so is not doing his job. Sometimes, if you have one or two very hard workers on the ship, they pull the others after them, and everything is done. If you do not have such a person, it is trouble. But there are fewer and fewer people now in the industry. If I have a problem, for example, with an engineer who is drinking too much, I call the company and they say, 'We don't have any more engineers; make do with what you have.' And there are many small problems. A passenger keeps going into the kitchen, for example, and the cook comes to me and says, 'I cannot have the passengers in the kitchen,' and I must go to the passenger and explain. Or the crew does not throw the Christmas tree overboard and there are needles everywhere and I must say, 'Please throw the tree overboard.' Or someone will want to watch one video and another will want to watch another video and they come to me and I must say, 'Tonight we watch this video, and tomorrow we watch the other video.' You see? It's kindergarten!" He says this with affectionate amusement.

"Now," he says, "I must go down to the bar and drink some champagne with the chief engineer, for fixing the reefer."

We descend to the bar and find Dedek, Appeldorn, Thomas, and Möschter seated at the bar. Behind the bar are Boden and Laschewski. The captain sits at the bar and opens a bottle of Austrian champagne. A toast is raised to the reefer. The captain reloads his pipe. He sits beneath a small circular lamp in the ceiling in a perfect cone of pipe smoke.

The presence of the captain seems to raise the spirits of the crew. Talk runs to women, ships, American politics. When the champagne is gone, Laschewski pours rum and Coke into a row of beer glasses over ice. Möschter produces a lemon from the galley, and Appeldorn cuts it into slices on the cover of a German car magazine. He drops a slice into each glass.

Appeldorn has been on four ships that have been boarded and robbed by pirates armed with automatic weapons. Möschter was on a ship where pirates robbed the captain of everything but the clothes on his back. Piracy is a fact of modern shipping. It is worst along the coasts of Asia and South America. Typically, they break into specific containers and make off with a boatload of boxes. Often armed, they are rarely violent. There are exceptions; in the mid-1980s a small container ship simply disappeared in the Red Sea. It didn't sink; there was no storm, no distress call. Not a single member of the crew was ever found. The ship was almost certainly hijacked, the crew dispatched overboard. This happened again in 1998, the captain tells me, when a tanker vanished without a trace.

From time to time, a passenger will jump overboard. Sometimes they leave notes in their cabins. In one case, there was no note, but a crewman found a pair of sandals by the rail the next morning.

When I was a small boy, aboard a ferry we took in the summers, I would climb the railing on deck and rest my chin between my hands. From that vantage, I would stare down into the boiling wake along the edge of the green water and grapple with my desire to jump off. The impulse to jump was strong, but not as strong as the desire to remain aboard. Twenty-five years later, here in the middle of the Atlantic late at night, I come alone and stand on the edge of the wing and watch the black water slide by. I watch the foaming wake of the ship, receding into the darkness beyond the range of the lights, and feel that same desire, low in the gut, to throw myself into the sea. It is not, at least consciously, a suicidal impulse. The ocean simply pulls. As I lean against the rail in the wind and gaze blankly at the water, I imagine that I've finally surrendered and leapt off.

I imagine the shock of the cold water, the swarm of bubbles, the roar of the engines. As I resurface, bobbing in the swell, the ship is already drawing away. It is then, in this fantasy, that I change my mind. I didn't mean it, I think. I strike out for the ship, shouting for help, but there is no one on deck. I imagine them all, asleep in their cabins or seated at the bar, every one of them ignorant of my mistake. The ship is moving at nearly twenty knots; I don't have a chance. In any case, there is nothing to grab. There is no line in the water, no ladder. I finally give up and tread water. I watch the ship recede until it is merely a cluster of yellow lights and realize that I'm going to die.

When I finally withdraw from the wing, into the warmth of the bridge, I register the dim lights of the console and the shadow of the watch officer, bending over his charts, with a deep stab of gratitude.

The captain finally leaves the bar. One after another, the men retire. "Last time we repaired a reefer and drank Bacardi," says Appeldorn. "Today we repair another reefer and drink champagne. Tomorrow," he deadpans, "I'm going to fuck up another reefer."

Late the following morning, Hinahon spots a whale off the starboard side, headed west. It is black-backed, thirty feet long. We move out to the edge of the wing and watch it pass. The whale provides company, of a kind, if only for a few minutes. As the days wear on, despite the presence of the crew and passengers, there is a growing sense onboard of isolation.

This is not entirely unpleasant, but it is strongest on the bridge, where you cannot dodge the impact of the open sea.

In what has become a daily ritual, I join Dedek, Glaser, Appeldorn, Boden, and Laschewski for coffee in the ship's office. As always, much of the break is spent in silence. They all smoke. Glaser stares absently at the tabletop and works his fingers through his beard. Appeldorn rests his elbow on the table, leans his head into his hand, and slowly rubs his forehead over his left eye. At the bar, in the evenings, they pick up. But here, in the harsh light of the office, each of them appears pale, bone-weary. There is a quality to their expressions, stronger in some than in others, of shellshock.

The officers do not seem to share this. And most of the Filipino crewmen, whether chipping rust on deck, swabbing oil in the engine room, or playing cards, are inscrutable. When greeted, they respond with smiles that reveal nothing. If they take any pleasure from their life at sea, or have tired of it, I am not able to tell.

We steam eastward, and the weather remains fair. I explore the ship. There are two miniature, salt-water swimming pools aboard, both empty. I find an operative wooden sauna, a laundry room, and a bleak, windowless exercise room equipped with a rowing machine, a stationary bike, and a Ping-Pong table. Far beneath the foredeck, down ladders and through hatches, is the ship's brig—a small steel pocket of the ship's hull recently converted by

Appeldorn into a barred cell. The cell awaits the next set of stowaways. Stowaways are frequently discovered aboard freighters of all kinds, almost invariably en route to America. Even if cooperative, stowaways present an enormous bureaucratic and logistical hassle for the crew that discovers them. Delivering them to authorities can delay a ship by many days, and innumerable forms must be filed. In ports with a history of stowaways, the upper decks are locked and a twenty-four-hour guard posted on the gangway to discourage them. They get aboard anyway, and unwelcome passengers are often to be found in the lifeboat. Before leaving every port in Europe, Africa, Asia, or South America, the *Senator*'s crew makes a thorough, forty-minute search of the unlocked areas of the ship. And while I cannot imagine the crew of the *Senator* resorting to such measures, it is common knowledge that stowaways are sometimes thrown overboard to their deaths.

There is ample time to read on a freighter, for there is none of the scheduled entertainment found on a cruise ship. Unless you have a private satellite phone, one of the minor blessings of being at sea on a freighter is that you can't check your e-mail, your cell phone doesn't work, and your electronic agenda is worth less than a deck of cards. For a substantial fee, you can send or receive faxes or phone calls from the ship's bridge.

On late afternoons, the passengers often meet for a drink before dinner. Passengers aboard freighters are usually individuals with long vacations or flexible schedules: school-teachers, writers, painters, retired professionals, the odd college student. Collivet and I were joined by three couples in Savannah.

The next day I sit at the bridge with Second Officer Raik Thomas. The youngest officer aboard at twenty-seven, Thomas is over six feet tall, thin and bearded, and in his spectacles he might be a graduate student in philos-ophy. Also from the former East Germany, Thomas is descended from a line of seafarers. His grandfather and father were both ship's captains. "One of the clearest mem-ories of my childhood," says Thomas, "is of my father going back to sea. I was five or six years old, and it was Christmas morning. He had just come home from his last voyage, and the company called on Christmas Eve. There was an emergency, and they asked if he would take the ship. At that time, it was still East Germany, and there were fences at the port. And when we dropped him off at the harbor—I was sitting in the back, watching through the window—he said goodbye to my mother, at the gate. As he went through, I could see him become ... It wasn't that he wanted to leave us; he and my mother were very close. He was a good father. I was very proud of him. But as he went through the fence, at the port, and was about to board his ship, he became . . . lighter. You could see it. His back was to us, but you could see it. He was going back to sea."

The weather never turns on the *Senator*; not this time. It is January, but we might as well be crossing in June. Around 1:30 P.M. on January 20, eight and a half days after leaving the mouth of the Savannah, Thomas spots it first. He and I and the captain are all studying the horizon through binoculars. "There," he says and points. "Spain."

A broad hill, barely perceptible through the haze, floats like a mirage in the far distance off the port bow. We are not far from the site of the Battle of Trafalgar, Admiral Lord Horatio Nelson's victorious engagement over the French and Spanish fleet in 1805. Twenty minutes later, the Atlas Mountains of Morocco loom into view to starboard. We pass through the Strait of Gibraltar, dense with ship traffic, accompanied by dolphins.

As we glide into the Mediterranean, the sun sinks into the Atlas Mountains, now astern. The captain paces restlessly on the upper deck, watching the sun. Finally he joins me on the starboard wing. Through binoculars, he studies the edge of the blood orange sun as it darkens and melts into the saddle between two peaks. This is my last chance to see the green flash; there were none during the crossing, and I will disembark in Valencia tomorrow. The sun sinks to its waist, its bottom losing shape and oozing in a liquid skirt over the ridge line. Finally, all at once, the sun's fine, orange crown pops from view behind the mountains. A moment later, a quick flash of color comes over the ridge.

"There!" the captain nearly shouts.

It is a pale explosion of light. But it's green. By God, it is green.

ON CANNON CLIFF

On a late winter morning in 1998, John Bouchard starts up
the steep snow slope at the base of the Black Dike, a 600-foot
gully of ice and rock that splits the broad granite face of New
Hampshire's Cannon Cliff like a hatchet wound. It is thirty
degrees, nearly windless, and a fine, dry snow falls through
the dense fog that conceals the summit. In its present, win-
try aspect, the cliff—which is nearly a mile wide, a thousand
feet high, and an average of ten degrees off vertical—resembles nothing more than the base of a north wall in the Alps.

From the foot of the Dike a talus field descends into beech trees. Farther lies a two-laned road. Half a mile away, Bouchard's truck stands alone in a parking lot.

Bouchard, a forty-six-year-old alpinist from neighboring North Conway, New Hampshire, climbs in plastic, neon-yellow boots. Steel crampons, their points freshly sharpened with a hand file, are secured to the boots' soles. In each gloved hand he carries an ice tool—or short-shafted, technical ice axe. Bouchard knows the route well; in 1971, then an unknown with two years of experience, he was the first person to climb it. The year before, Yvon Chouinard, the godfather of American ice climbing, proclaimed the unclimbed gully "the last great plum in the East," believing the route to lie beyond the technical standards of the day. The Dike was quickly acknowledged as the country's most challenging line on ice, and the details of Bouchard's first ascent—solo, a broken ice axe, a lost glove, finishing at night in a storm—established his reputation, at the age of nineteen, as one of the country's preeminent ice climbers.

Bouchard went on to complete a number of landmark climbs in the Alps and elsewhere, including the first ascent of the Grand Charmoz North Couloir, in Chamonix, France, in 1975. In 1981, he and partner Mark Richey climbed the north face of Switzerland's Eiger in fifteen hours, then the second-fastest ascent of the infamous wall. Bouchard abandoned climbing for parapenting in 1987 and spent six years competing and designing paragliders. The number-one-ranked paraglider pilot in the United States in 1990 and 1991, he returned to climbing full time in 1993. In 1996, Bouchard and Richey made a long-awaited second ascent, in six days, of the East Pillar of India's Shivling peak. Since an epic, twelve-day first ascent of the route in 1981, not a single attempt on the high-altitude route had succeeded. They trained for the climb, in winter, on Cannon Cliff.

Twenty-seven years after its first ascent, the Black Dike is still widely considered to be the finest alpine climb in New England. And while the Dike's objective challenges have retreated considerably before advancing skills and technology, world-class climbers the likes of Neil Beidelman (the guide whose efforts saved several lives in the Hall and Fischer disaster on Everest in 1996) can often be found in the parking lot, gearing up for the route on a snowy morning.

I have asked Bouchard to run me through a three-day training program covering the vertical ice and alpine techniques used on high-altitude walls. With Bouchard in the lead, we plan to ascend a handful of the region's classic alpine winter routes—commonly a mix of ice, snow, and rock. On such climbs, in late winter, we may also encounter what Scottish winter climbers embrace as "full conditions," or bad weather. On Cannon, says Bouchard, an alpinist in training can find routes as technically challenging—albeit much shorter—as anything to be found on the world's most notorious faces: Cerro Torre, for example, or Shivling's East Pillar.

"Cannon has everything," Bouchard argues, "except altitude. You can practice on snowed-up rock in crampons, mixed ice and rock, and technical rock climbing, all on a single route in varying conditions." Like the Eiger itself—whose notorious, crumbling north wall has haunted generations of climbers—the New Hampshire cliff is feared for instability and rock fall. At least four climbers have been killed upon its face. Mount Washington, an hour to the north, is called the most dangerous small mountain in the world, thanks largely to its avalanche danger, freezing temperatures, and blistering winds (231-mile-per-hour gusts have been clocked at the summit, the highest winds recorded anywhere in the world at a fixed location). For high-altitude climbers in training, however, the winter conditions on Washington, Cannon, and other regional crags are ideal. "If you train in bad conditions," Bouchard explains, "you're less surprised when they hit at higher altitudes."

Up on the Dike, Bouchard quickly finishes the first pitch, or rope length—generally in the neighborhood of 150 feet—and sets a belay anchor. At this stage the climbing is straightforward, and I have soon joined him at the base of the route's crux, or most difficult section, a short rock buttress bare of ice.

Bouchard leaves the safety of the belay ledge and scrapes out across the rock. I belay, feeding the rope through a device affixed to my harness as he proceeds. He spirals out and up toward a section of snow and ice, perches the points of his crampons on small ledges, grasps knobs of rock with ungloved hands. For the moment, his ice tools rest in holsters at his waist. He pauses, clips his rope into a piton, and climbs on. He is less than eight feet from me, weighting a handhold, when a rock the size of a toolbox comes loose in his hand. The rock misses his boot by inches and skips down the gully. Luckily, we are alone on the route. Bouchard teeters for a moment on his crampons—for an instant I am sure he will recover—and plunges from the face.

It is a short fall, easily belayed, but it surprises me. Bouchard is one of the world's most experienced alpinists, at home on a route he pioneered—a climb he has frequently third-classed, or climbed unroped—and it is easy to forget, on some level, that he might actually rely on my belay.

"There is an element of randomness that you can't control," Bouchard says later of such alpine routes. "But part of the pleasure is knowing that you're willing to take that chance. It's very different from the risks taken by the Everest crowd, on the one hand, or by bungee jumpers. The risks on Everest are high, but totally out of the climber's control; the actual climbing takes very little skill. Bungee jumping is the reverse; nothing can go wrong if you do it right."

The bare rock crux notwithstanding, most of the Black Dike is sheathed in ice—tinted ochre by minerals in the groundwater—and offers challenges well suited to the intermediate ice climber. Like rock climbing, ice climbing has seen a tremendous boom in participation in recent years. In

1980, Bouchard estimates, there may have been something in the neighborhood of 1,500 regular ice climbers in the United States. At this writing, that figure stands above 10,000.

Hooking and swinging with our tools, toe-kicking up narrow chimneys of ice, we finish the route without further incident. As I follow Bouchard, climbing at the outside edge of my ability through secondary cruxes, I try to imagine finding myself on the same terrain, alone, unroped and with a single, primitive ice axe, with no idea what lay ahead and no choice but to continue, on that winter evening in 1971. Not a chance, I think. When I finally top out into the trees, I shake his hand and congratulate him. We hike off the back of the cliff through the snow and drive to a neighboring village for lunch. I am elated from the climb, but Bouchard is pensive, and the conversation soon turns to mortality.

"The first time I helped carry a body off a mountain, it was tough," he says. "After that it didn't really bother me. But they were strangers. I never had a friend die with me on a climb. They just went away on expeditions and never came back."

In the summer of 1994, Bouchard went to a dinner party in Chamonix. It was a reunion of sorts, and the climbers, all in their forties or early fifties, sat around a long table on a porch across a valley from the Chamonix Aiguilles and spoke of the dead. Of Bouchard's original circle, some fifteen British, French, and American climbers who had gotten their starts together in the Alps in the early 1970s and become friends, some half had been killed in the mountains. In cases, survivors at the party had been with them, climbing, when the accidents occurred. In every case, they were killed by what climbers call "objective dangers"—hazards largely or entirely outside their control. World-class alpinists all, they were lost to high-altitude exhaustion, collapsing seracs, avalanches, crevasses, rock fall. This was the first time that some of the survivors had met since the accidents, and as the evening wore on, the dead climbers became almost palpable in the empty chairs.

Bouchard has climbed as hard as any of his peers, and his six-year sabbatical in paragliding was a good deal more dangerous, statistically speaking, than alpinism. He broke an ankle once, high on Cannon, and finished the climb. Later, he was struck by lightning, near the summit of the Walker Spur on the Grandes Jorasses. High on the Gervasutti Pillar in the Alps, he was once caught in a hail of falling rocks. For half a minute, blocks ranging in size from baseballs to refrigerators roared down the face in a dense cloud of dust. With no cover, Bouchard had no choice but to lower his head and wait. When it ended, a climber in another party—ten feet from Bouchard—was dead. Bouchard and his partner were unscathed.

While rationally aware of the risks, he claims to actively cultivate a sense of denial. There is also professional pressure to consistently push limits.

"Once you're in it," he explains, "you become very, very

competitive. As a climber, a first ascent is your work. And like an artist, you need to produce."

A National Merit Scholar in high school, Bouchard went on to earn a degree in medieval studies from the University of Vermont. "In college," he says, "I was fascinated by the Crusades, by the Knights Templar. I felt that I had been given a calling; that I was put here to climb. I had the sense, when I was climbing, of fulfilling a greater obligation." Raised Roman Catholic, Bouchard prays before significant climbs. He admits that he has experienced something like a state of grace on long, difficult routes, among them his solo first ascent of the Grand Charmoz. While some of his peers aggressively deny the role of faith or superstition in climbing, Bouchard has found that most alpinists—novices and experts alike—carry talismans of some kind or another and are willing to participate in impromptu religious ceremonies at the start of expeditions. These observances are often a mix of local custom and various Western prayers.

The following day finds us back at Cannon, scratching our way up the mixed ice, snow, and rock of *Wiessner's Direct*. I have little experience on mixed terrain, and the climbing becomes rapidly more desperate as we proceed. We are not climbing, as alpinists are often forced, through subzero temperatures and heavy snow. But it is inarguably winter, and cold. Because many of the moves require standard rock-climbing holds, we climb ungloved, our ice tools often holstered at our waists. The flakes and ledges of rock are often dusted if not blanketed with snow that must be brushed away with bare fingertips. While attaining the foot of a steep triangular snowfield, I have no choice but to plunge a blue hand deep into the surface powder and cling to the crusted snow beneath. At rests, I snap my hands to drive the blood back into the fingertips. In other sections, following Bouchard's unhurried example, I experiment with the tools. There is ice on the route, and ice requires crampons, but since much of the rock is bare, much of the climbing is dry-tooling—hooking and wedging the picks and heads of the ice tools in rocky cracks, perching our crampon points on granite ledges sometimes no wider than a thumbnail clipping. Some of the slabs and holds are glazed with rime ice. This fine, transparent veneer is too slick for a grasping hand and too thin to support pick or crampons. Such terrain is often unclimbable, and alpinists must seek another way.

Here and there, tucked in cracks, sturdy tongues of water ice allow reliable crampon and tool placements, and for one or two moves we are actually ice climbing. Then we're off onto rock and snow again, mixing holds, pausing to consider choices. Deliberate or intuitive, there is puzzle-solving— move by move—in all technical climbing; the variables only increase on mixed terrain.

Near the conclusion of the third pitch, as I wedge the heads of my ice tools in a tapering vertical crack above my head, it occurs to me that my adze—a bowed crescent of honed steel, sharp enough to peel a potato and designed to clear hard ice from a potential anchor position—is perfectly poised, should the placement blow out suddenly under my weight, to strike me in the face. As I weight the tools and prepare to move up with my crampons, I reflect on this possibility aloud. "It happens all the time," Bouchard remarks offhandedly from his belay position. "A partner of mine had an adze go though the bridge of his nose. It shattered his eye orbit, nearly blinded him."

"Thanks," I tell him, easing up to a higher position on my crampons, out of the weapon's arc.

Bouchard wears a canary yellow climbing jacket. Waterproof, streamlined, devoid of straps, buckles and extra zippers, it is his latest design for Wild Things, Inc., the company he founded in 1981 in North Conway with Marie Meunier, also a climber and then his wife.

"The best climbing gear looks too simple to be appealing to many nonexperts," Bouchard said earlier in the parking lot. "Many of the bigger companies manufacture equipment and clothing that has the climbing look but is actually too heavy and impractical for technical climbing. One company makes a suit covered with gear clips and extra pockets and double zippers. It sells, because it looks hardcore and nonprofessionals don't know better. But no serious climbers I know would ever wear it."

He gestures at my shell, an industry classic that many climbers swear by. "That jacket's heavier than it needs to be. You take a climber's equipment: clothes, boots, tools, rack. Unless you're manic about weight, it really adds up. A few extra ounces here, a couple there. It's invisible, but pretty soon you're carrying ten or fifteen extra pounds. On a long climb—even three extra pounds can kill you."

Bouchard quotes Antoine de Saint-Exupéry on aircraft design: "Perfection is finally attained not when there is no longer anything to add, but when there is no longer anything to take away." Driven by this philosophy, many of the designs at Wild Things have won awards in the climbing industry.

High on *Wiessner's*, when I have switched places with Bouchard on the next ledge, he sets out across a broad, featureless granite slab, headed for a crack at the foot of an overhanging wall. He has twenty-five feet to travel, and in summer, in sticky rubber rock shoes, the angle of the slab—something in the neighborhood of twenty degrees—would be as easy to traverse as a sun porch. In winter, for a climber in crampons, it becomes a different proposition. There is nothing to hold, no crack in which to secure an anchor, and the angle is just steep enough, as Bouchard continues, his knees bent slightly, creeping out across the stone, to make the crampons slide a quarter inch at every second or third step. The narrow belay ledge lies three feet below the edge of the slab. The slab ends at my waist, and should Bouchard fall, he will come off. There is no way, I realize, that he could stop the momentum of his fall. He will come into me, complete with crampons and ice tools, or over me, should I duck behind the ledge, and either way the anchor will sustain a shock. I glance quickly back and down the nearly vertical wall behind me. Flakes and horns of rock protrude from the main face. There is nothing beneath me that anyone should like to fall on, rope or no rope. My responsibility—at this moment the sole reason, really, for my existence—is to make sure he falls no farther from the anchor than the rope that he has taken out. Conceivably, I could rope in a few feet as he rolls. Should he fall, I decide, I will duck. A crampon in the face or belay hand, beyond its immediate discomfort, would seriously endanger the belay, with potentially fatal results. I'll drop behind the ledge, try to take in some rope, let him roll over me, and hope for the best. I consider the anchor, two pitons hammered into a crack, knee-high, and wonder of there's any chance it could blow.

Bouchard takes several creeping, precise steps, as if walking on a windowpane, before he begins to slide. The steel points of the crampons growling on the granite, he slides an inch, two, three, and finally comes to a halt, the points catching on minute granules. He waits for a moment and then carefully steps forward again with one foot. He shifts his weight. It holds. He picks up and replaces his opposing foot. Step by step he inches closer to the crack and safety. Twice more he begins to slide and stops, each time proceeding a bit farther. The farther away from me he gets, the more rope is out, the faster and farther he will fall on the anchor, and the more uncomfortable, watching him, I become. Finally he reaches the crack, gets a piece in. He clips in the rope. It's done.

For the follower, traversing the slab is nothing. In my case, the anchor is above me. If I slide, the rope will stop me. If I fall, I'll just get up. There, in essence, is the difference between leading and seconding.

By the end of the route—pawing with my crampons, flailing and hooking with the tools, hanging shamelessly to rest on Bouchard's belay—I've abandoned anything approaching decent form. For a climber at my level, the *Black Dike* was a perfect challenge. But the upper stretches of *Wiessner's Direct*—at least in winter conditions—are beyond me. It doesn't help that the route's crux—a nasty granite fin and then a chimney—is the climb's conclusion. I get up it, just barely, with Bouchard reeling me in like a tarpon. Exhausted and jumpy, my nerves shot, I'm eager to get off the 600-foot cliff and down to a warm bar and a meal. As Bouchard coils the rope, a fine snow falling in the dusk, he puts the climb in broader perspective: "On a big alpine wall like the Eiger, you have to climb that kind of terrain over and over. Some of the pitches will be a little easier, some of them harder. But most of it will be about like that. Thirty, forty pitches. Twelve or fifteen hours a day. And then, twenty pitches up, you can always get hit by a storm."

In a 1977 French journal entitled *Les Grands de la Montagne*, the young John Bouchard was listed among the most promising alpinists of his generation. During my visit, while thumbing through his copy of the journal, I came across this list. By no means conclusive, it numbered nine climbers from three nations. Of the nine names on the list, five are marked with simple crosses, inscribed in pen over the years.